Reading Skills Competency Tests

THIRD LEVEL

Walter B. Barbe, Ph.D.

A nationally-known authority in the areas of reading and learning disabilities, Walter B. Barbe, Ph.D., is editor-in-chief of the widely acclaimed magazine, *Highlights for Children,* and adjunct professor at The Ohio State University. Dr. Barbe is the author of over 150 professional articles and a number of books, including *Personalized Reading Instruction* (West Nyack, NY: Parker Publishing Co., Inc., 1975), coauthored with Jerry L. Abbott. He is also the senior author and editor of two series: *Creative Growth with Handwriting* (Columbus, Ohio: Zaner-Bloser, Inc., 1975) and the *Barbe Reading Skills Check Lists and Activities* (West Nyack, NY: The Center for Applied Research in Education, Inc., 1976). Dr. Barbe is a fellow of the American Psychological Association and is listed in *Who's Who in America* and *American Men of Science.*

Henriette L. Allen, Ph.D.

Henriette L. Allen, Ph.D., a former classroom teacher in the Coventry, Rhode Island, schools, Aramco Schools of Dhahran, Saudi Arabia, and The American Community School of Benghazi, Libya, is presently an administrative assistant to the superintendent with the Jackson, Mississippi, Public Schools. She has taught reading skills at elementary and secondary levels and supervised the development of a Continuous Progress Reading Program for the Jackson Public Schools. Dr. Allen has lectured widely in the fields of reading, classroom management, and leadership in educational administration. She is listed in the *World Who's Who of Women* and *Who's Who—School District Officials.*

Wiley C. Thornton, M.Ed.

Wiley C. Thornton, M.Ed., has many years' experience in classroom teaching and educational testing and is presently research assistant in the Jackson Public Schools. His responsibilities include project evaluations, report writings, upgrading of teacher skills in interpretation and use of educational research, as well as test construction. Mr. Thornton is a frequent consultant and speaker to teacher, parent, and civic groups on educational measurement, testing, and test construction and use.

COMPETENCY TESTS FOR BASIC READING SKILLS

The Center for Applied Research in Education, Inc.
West Nyack, New York 10994

Permission is given for individual classroom teachers and reading specialists to reproduce the student test pages for individual or classroom use. Reproduction of these materials for an entire school or school system is strictly forbidden.

Printed in the United States of America

About the *Competency Tests for Basic Reading Skills*

The Reading Skills Competency Tests are a practical tool designed to provide classroom teachers, reading specialists, Title I teachers and others an inventory of those reading skills mastered and those which need to be taught. The tests can be used at all levels with any reading program, as they test mastery of specific reading skills at particular levels.

For easy use, the test materials are organized into eight distinct units tailored to evaluate children's reading skills at each of the following expectancy and difficulty levels:

Reading Skills Competency Tests: READINESS LEVEL
Reading Skills Competency Tests: FIRST LEVEL
Reading Skills Competency Tests: SECOND LEVEL
Reading Skills Competency Tests: THIRD LEVEL
Reading Skills Competency Tests: FOURTH LEVEL
Reading Skills Competency Tests: FIFTH LEVEL
Reading Skills Competency Tests: SIXTH LEVEL
Reading Skills Competency Tests: ADVANCED LEVEL

The tests give reading teachers a quick, informal means to measure the mastery of reading objectives. They can be used at any time to assess the student's competence in specific reading skills, to pinpoint specific skill weaknesses and problems, and to plan appropriate corrective or remedial instruction in an individualized reading program.

The sequence of the tests corresponds to the sequence of the well-known "Barbe Reading Skills Check Lists," which provide a complete developmental skill sequence from Readiness through Advanced Levels. Each level-unit presents ready-to-use informal tests for evaluating all skills that are listed on the Skills Check List at that level. Tests can be administered individually or to a group by a teacher or a paraprofessional.

Each unit of test materials contains:

1. Directions for using the Reading Skills Competency Tests at that grade level to identify individual reading needs and prescribe appropriate instruction.
2. Copies of the Skills Check List and a Group Summary Profile at that grade level for use in individual and group recordkeeping.
3. Reading Skills Competency Tests for assessing all skills at that particular grade level, including teacher test sheets with directions and answer keys for administering and evaluating each test plus reproducible student test sheets.

About the Competency Tests for Basic Reading Skills

Note: The student test sheets are also available from the publisher on duplicating masters.

4. A duplicating master of the Skills Check List at the particular grade level for setting up individual skills records for all children in a class.
5. A copy of the "Barbe Reading Skills Sequential Skill Plan" chart.

For easiest use of the materials, complete directions are provided in each unit for using the Competency Tests at that level and for recording the information on the student skills Check List and the Group Summary Profile.

The test items in each level unit correspond to the skills indicated on the Check List. The Check List can be marked to indicate which skills the child has mastered or the skills in which further instruction is needed. The Group Summary Profile can be used to obtain an overall picture of class progress and to identify the skills which need to be taught. It is also useful in identifying small groups with similar needs, students who require personalized help on a prerequisite skill, and students who need continued help on a current skill.

You will find that these tests provide for:

- quick, informal assessment of students' competence in reading skills
- diagnosis and prescription of specific reading skill weaknesses and needs
- devising of appropriate teaching strategies for individuals and small or large groups
- continuous evaluation of each child's progress in the basic reading skills
- flexibility in planning the reading instructional program
- immediate feedback to the student and the teacher

The Competency Tests for Basic Reading Skills can be used by all reading teachers in either a self-contained classroom or a team setting. They are as flexible as the teacher chooses to make them. Hopefully, they will provide an efficient, systematic means to identify the specific reading skills that students need to learn and thus meet to a greater degree, their individual reading needs.

Henriette L. Allen

Walter B. Barbe

Contents

About the Competency Tests for Basic Reading Skills 3

How to Use the Competency Tests and Check List 9

Begin at the Beginning • 9
Recording on the Check List • 10
Conferencing with the Pupil • 11
Conferencing with Parents • 11
Conferencing with Professional Staff • 11
Providing Check Lists to the Next Grade Level Teacher • 11
Making a Group Summary Profile from Individual Check Lists • 11
Ensuring the Sequential Presentation of Skills • 12
Using the Sequential Skill Plan Chart • 12

Reading Skills Check List–Third Level 13

Group Summary Profile–Third Level 15

Reading Skills Competency Tests: Third Level 19

I. VOCABULARY

A. *Recognizes 220 Dolch Basic Sight Words* • 20, 22, 24, 26, 28

B. *Word Meaning:* • 30

1 Comprehension and Use of Words • 30
a. Function Words • 30
b. Direction Words • 32
c. Action Words • 34
d. Forms of Address • 36
e. Career Words • 38
f. Color Words • 40
g. Metric Words • 42
h. Curriculum Words • 44, 46

Contents

II. WORD ANALYSIS

A. *Refine Phonics Skills* • 48

1. All Initial Consonant Sounds • 48, 50
2. Short and Long Vowel Sounds • 52
3. Changes in Words • 54
   a. Adding s, es, d, ed, ing, er, est • 54
   b. Dropping Final e and Adding ing • 56
   c. Doubling the Consonant before Adding ing • 58
   d. Changing y to i Before Adding es • 60
4. Vowel Rules • 62
   a. Vowel in One-Syllable Word Is Short • 62
   b. Vowel in a Syllable or Word Ending in e Is Long • 64
   c. Two Vowels Together, First Is Often Long and Second Is Silent • 66
   d. Vowel Alone in Word Is Short • 68
5. C Followed by i, e, y Makes s Sound • 70
   C Followed by a, o, u Makes k Sound • 70
6. G Followed by i, e, y Makes j Sound • 72
   G Followed by a, o, u Makes guh Sound • 72
7. Silent Letters in kn, wr, gn • 74

B. *Knows Skills of:* • 76

1. Forming Plurals by Adding s, es, ies, and by Changing f to v and Adding es • 76, 78
2. Similarities of Sound such as x and cks • 80
3. Can Read Roman Numerals I, V, X • 82

C. *Syllabication Rules* • 84

1. There Are Usually as Many Syllables in a Word as There Are Vowels • 84
2. When There Is a Single Consonant Between Two Vowels, the Vowel Goes with the First Syllable • 86
3. When There Is a Double Consonant, the Syllable Break Is Between the Two Consonants and One Is Silent • 88

D. *Can Hyphenate Words Using Syllable Rules* • 90

E. *Understands Use of Primary Accent Mark* • 92

F. *Knows to Accent First Syllable, Unless It Is a Prefix, Otherwise Accent Second Syllable* • 94

III. COMPREHENSION

A. *Can Find Main Idea in a Story* • 96

B. *Can Keep Events in Proper Sequence* • 98

C. *Can Draw Logical Conclusions* • 100

D. *Is Able to See Relationships* • 102

E. *Can Predict Outcomes* • 104

F. *Can Follow Printed Directions* • 106

G. *Can Read for a Definite Purpose* • 108

1. For Pleasure • 108
2. To Obtain Answer to Question • 110
3. To Obtain General Idea of Content • 112

H. *Classify Items* • 114

I. *Use Index* • 116

J. *Alphabetize Words by First Two Letters* • 118

K. *Knows Technique of Skimming* • 120

L. *Can Determine What Source to Obtain Information* • 122

M. *Use Maps and Charts* • 124

IV. ORAL AND SILENT READING

A. *Oral Reading* • 126

1. Reads with Expression • 126
2. Comprehends Material Read Aloud • 128

B. *Silent Reading* • 132

1. Reads Silently without Finger Pointing and Lip Movement • 132
2. Comprehends Material Read Silently • 134
3. Reads Faster Silently Than Orally • 138

C. *Listening* • 140

1. Comprehends Material Read Aloud by Another • 140
2. Can Follow Directions Read Aloud • 142

Barbe Reading Skills Check List–Third Level (Duplicating Master)

Barbe Reading Skills Check List Sequential Skill Plan (Chart)

How to Use the Competency Tests and Check List

A major task for teachers is verifying mastery of basic skills and keeping records. Recordkeeping and competency tests are of greater concern today than ever before. But knowing of their necessity does not make the task any easier. Competency tests and the accompanying records may be compared to a road map. One must drive through Town B to reach Town W. Competency tests are designed to assist you in verifying mastery of basic reading skills, and to indicate where to begin on the journey of reading mastery. The Reading Skills Check Lists provide check points to verify (1) where the student is on the sequence of skills, (2) when the skills were mastered, and (3) at what rate he or she is progressing.

In order for skills to develop sequentially, it is vital that we have an idea of where a student is within the sequence of reading skills. The Reading Skills Competency Tests and Check List in this unit are designed to help you teach directly to identified student needs, on a day-to-day, week-to-week, and month-to-month basis.

The Reading Skills Competency Tests are easy-to-administer tests for each reading skill on the "Barbe Reading Skills Check Lists." Directions for administering each test are given on a teacher page. This page also provides the answer key and the number of correct responses needed for mastery. Facing the teacher page is the student test page, which can be used as a master for copying when reproduction for classroom use is via copy machine. The student tests are also available on spirit duplicating masters.

The Check Lists are not intended as a rigid program for reading instruction. Rather they are meant to provide a general pattern around which a program may be built. The Third Level Skills Check List is divided into four major headings: Vocabulary, Word Analysis, Comprehension, and Oral and Silent Reading. Each area is of great importance to the student's development. In presenting the skills on the Check List, it is recommended that you deal alternately with some activities from each of the four major headings.

You will find a copy of the Third Level Skills Check List on page 14, and a duplicating master of the Check List at the end of this aid, which you can copy and use for individual recordkeeping.

Begin at the Beginning

Before planning an instructional program for any pupil, it is necessary to determine at what level the student is reading. This may be determined through the use of an informal reading inventory. It is then necessary to identify which basic reading skills the pupil has mastered and which skills need remediation or initial teaching.

The Competency Tests for Basic Reading Skills offer a quick, practical means to determine which skills the student has mastered and on which the student needs additional work. It is suggested that the tests be administered at the beginning of a school year. The tests may also be used at any time throughout the year to determine a student's entry point in a Reading Skills Class, or to reevaluate the progress of individual students. The tests may be given to a large group, a small group, or an individual, whichever is appropriate for those being tested and for the test being administered. Some tests, such as Oral Reading, must be administered individually. The entry point into the reading program should be at that point when a student begins to encounter difficulty with a particular reading skill.

The tests may be used as a pre test to indicate where instruction is needed, and the same tests may also be used as a post test to indicate mastery or non-mastery. Once a pupil's areas of difficulty are identified, you may then plan instructional activities accordingly. After the student has worked through a unit of instruction, you may use the same test to verify mastery of the skill. When mastery occurs, the student is advanced to another skill. When the student is unsuccessful on the specific test item, additional instruction is needed. If a reasonable amount of instruction does not result in mastery, it may be that changing instructional approaches is needed or that more work is needed on earlier skills.

Once you have decided the level of mastery tests needed, the assessing part of the reading program is ready to begin. Specific directions are given for each test. At the Third Level, you may assign the test to be taken and permit the students to work independently. The directions are given at the top of every student test page. In some instances, as in oral reading, you may have to test each student individually.

Recording on the Check List

Recordkeeping is an important part in any instructional design. Simplicity and ease is vital. One effective method for marking the Skills Check List is as follows:

B. Knows skills of:			
1. Forming plurals			
by adding s, es, ies	10/11	10/16	M
by changing f to v and adding es	M	10/19	
2. Similarities of sound such as x and cks	10/23	M	
3. Can read Roman numerals I, V, X	M		
C. Syllabication rules			
1. There are usually as many syllables in a word as there are vowels	10/30		
2. Where there is a single consonant between two vowels, the vowel goes with the first syllable			
3. When there is a double consonant, the syllable break is between the two consonants and one is silent			

Put an M in the first column if the pupil takes a test and demonstrates mastery of that basic reading skill. If the pupil has not mastered the skill, record the date. The date in column one indicates when instruction in the skill began. When the pupil is tested a second time, put an M in the second column if mastery is achieved, and record the date of mastery in the third column. Thus, anyone looking at the Check List can tell if the student mastered the skill before instruction or when instruction began, and when the skill was actually mastered. The Check List provides a written record of: (1) where the student is on the sequence of reading skills, (2) when the student mastered the skills, and (3) at what rate the student is progressing.

Conferencing with the Pupil

The student and teacher may discuss performance on the Competency Tests and Check List and jointly plan subsequent instruction. The Check List provides a guide for this discussion.

Conferencing with Parents

The Reading Skills Check List also serves as a guide for parent conferences. Using the Check List you can talk with parents about specific skills mastered, as well as those which have been taught but not yet fully mastered. Use of the Check List reassures parents of your concern for skill instruction, your knowledge of ways to aid their child in becoming a better reader, and of your professional plan which considers each child individually.

Conferencing with Professional Staff

Conferences with other staff such as school psychologists, counselors, and principals concerning an individual child's reading progress should focus on the instructional plan. When Check Lists are used, other professional staff members are provided with a written record of the teacher's progress and the child's progress in this program. The Check List provides information on the skills mastered, and when the skills were mastered.

Providing Check Lists to the Next Grade Level Teacher

One of the great problems in teaching reading skills at the beginning of the year is to know where to begin. If the Reading Skills Check Lists are passed along from class to class, the new teacher will know the skill level of every student in the room.

Making a Group Summary Profile from Individual Check Lists

While the Reading Skills Check List is intended primarily for individual use, there are various reasons for bringing together a record of the instructional needs to the entire class. In planning classroom strategies, you will find the use of the Group Profile on pages 16 and 17 helpful.

After you have recorded the skill level for each student on the Reading Skills Check List, you may then enter this information on the Group Profile. The Group Summary Profile is designed to help you identify groups of students who need a particular skill. It is a visual representation of the instructional needs of the entire class. It also presents the specific strengths and achievement levels of individual students.

The Group Profile may be used in conferences with supervisors and administrators to discuss the status of a particular class, the point of initial instruction, and the progress made to date. A different colored pen or pencil may be used to indicate the different grading or marking periods of the school year. This further indicates the progress the pupils have made within these periods of time.

The Group Profile can indicate the instructional materials and supplies which are needed. Since specific reading skills needs will be clearly identified, materials may be purchased which meet these needs.

Ensuring the Sequential Presentation of Skills

One of the goals of reading instruction is to develop a love of reading. But if students are to develop a love of reading, they must be able to read with efficiency. And in order to be efficient readers they must have at their ready command all of the necessary skills, including the ability to unlock new words and to read rapidly.

If the skills are to be mastered, they must be presented sequentially. When skills are presented out of sequence, critical skills are in danger of being bypassed or given minimal attention.

In many instances, the sequence of skills is firmly established; in other instances the sequence is less rigid. In these Check Lists, the skills have been placed in the order the authors feel is logical. Teachers should be free to change this sequence when there is reason to do so, being careful not to eliminate the presentation of the skill.

It is important that some skill instruction be conducted in groups. This prevents individual students from becoming isolated, a danger which sometimes occurs when too much individualization is undertaken.

Using the Sequential Skill Plan Chart

The importance of viewing the total sequential skills program cannot be minimized. The chart is intended primarily for use by the classroom teacher. If a personalized approach is used in teaching reading skills, it is still essential that the teacher view the skills as a continuous progression rather than as skills for a specific grade level. This chart allows the teacher to view not only those skills that are taught principally at the present grade placement, but also those skills which will be taught as the student progresses.

As an inservice tool, the chart provides teachers with the opportunity to see their own positions in the skills progression. It should be understood, of course, that there are any number of reasons why decisions may be made to teach the skills at levels different from those indicated on the chart. But it is important that reading skills be taught, and that basically they be taught in a sequential manner, in a planned reading program. Incidental teaching of reading skills often results in vital skills being neglected, or being bypassed until the student encounters difficulties. At that point, having to go back to earlier skills is more difficult and less effective.

The chart also provides administrators, supervisors, and teachers with direction for a total skills program.

Reading Skills Check List—Third Level

On the following pages you will find a copy of the "Barbe Reading Skills Check List–Third Level." The Check List presents a sequential outline of the skills to be mastered at this level in four major areas: Vocabulary, Word Analysis, Comprehension, and Oral and Silent Reading.

For use in individual recordkeeping, the Third Level Skills Check List is also printed on a spirit duplicating master at the end of this unit.

Accompanying the unit is a copy of the "Barbe Reading Skills Check List Sequential Skill Plan." This chart provides a visual representation of the total reading skills progression through all levels, including:

Readiness Level
First Level
Second Level
Third Level
Fourth Level
Fifth Level
Sixth Level
Advanced Level

BARBE READING SKILLS CHECK LIST
THIRD LEVEL

(Last Name) ____ (First Name) ____ (Name of School) ____

(Age) ____ (Grade Placement) ____ (Name of Teacher) ____

I. Vocabulary:

A. Recognizes Dolch 220 Basic Sight Words

___ a	___ done	___ I	___ out	___ these
___ about	___ don't	___ if	___ over	___ they
___ after	___ down	___ in	___ own	___ think
___ again	___ draw	___ into	___ pick	___ this
___ all	___ drink	___ is	___ play	___ those
___ always	___ eat	___ it	___ please	___ three
___ am	___ eight	___ its	___ pretty	___ to
___ an	___ every	___ jump	___ pull	___ today
___ and	___ fall	___ just	___ put	___ together
___ any	___ far	___ keep	___ ran	___ too
___ are	___ fast	___ kind	___ read	___ try
___ around	___ find	___ know	___ red	___ two
___ as	___ first	___ laugh	___ ride	___ under
___ ask	___ five	___ let	___ right	___ up
___ at	___ fly	___ light	___ round	___ upon
___ ate	___ for	___ like	___ run	___ us
___ away	___ found	___ little	___ said	___ use
___ be	___ four	___ live	___ saw	___ very
___ because	___ from	___ long	___ say	___ walk
___ been	___ full	___ look	___ see	___ want
___ before	___ funny	___ made	___ seven	___ warm
___ best	___ gave	___ make	___ shall	___ was
___ better	___ get	___ many	___ she	___ wash
___ big	___ give	___ may	___ show	___ we
___ black	___ go	___ me	___ sing	___ well
___ blue	___ goes	___ much	___ sit	___ went
___ both	___ going	___ must	___ six	___ were
___ bring	___ good	___ my	___ sleep	___ what
___ brown	___ got	___ myself	___ small	___ when
___ but	___ green	___ never	___ so	___ where
___ buy	___ grow	___ new	___ some	___ which
___ by	___ had	___ no	___ soon	___ white
___ call	___ has	___ not	___ start	___ who
___ came	___ have	___ now	___ stop	___ why
___ can	___ he	___ of	___ take	___ will
___ carry	___ help	___ off	___ tell	___ wish
___ clean	___ her	___ old	___ ten	___ with
___ cold	___ here	___ on	___ thank	___ work
___ come	___ him	___ once	___ that	___ would
___ could	___ his	___ one	___ the	___ write
___ cut	___ hold	___ only	___ their	___ yellow
___ did	___ hot	___ open	___ them	___ yes
___ do	___ how	___ or	___ then	___ you
___ does	___ hurt	___ our	___ there	___ your

B. Word Meaning:

1. Comprehends and uses correctly the following words:

a. Function Words
—against
—also
—being
—during
—each
—end
—enough
—men
—more
—most
—other
—same
—should
—since
—such
—than
—though
—thought
—through
—while
—women

b. Direction Words
—around
—backward
—forward
—left
—right
—toward

c. Action Words
—carry
—draw
—kick
—push
—skate
—swim
—think
—throw
—travel

d. Forms of Address
—Miss
—Mr.
—Mrs.
—Ms.

e. Career Words
—artist
—factory
—lawyer
—mechanic
—money
—nurse
—office
—operator
—teacher
—training
—vocation

f. Color Words
—brown
—green
—orange
—purple

g. Metric Words
—centigrade
—gram
—liter
—meter

h. Curriculum Words
—add
—American
—country
—ecology
—even
—fall
—few
—greater
—less
—number
—odd
—seasons
—set
—space
—spring
—state
—subtract
—summer
—United States
—winter
—world

II. Word Analysis:

A. Refine phonics skills:
1. All initial consonant sounds
2. Short and long vowel sounds
3. Changes in words by:
   a. adding s, es, d, ed, ing, er, est
   b. dropping final e and adding ing
   c. doubling the consonant before adding ing
   d. changing y to i before adding es
4. Vowel rules
   a. vowel in one-syllable word is short
   b. vowel in syllable or word ending in e is long
   c. two vowels together, first is often long and second is silent
   d. vowel alone in word is short
5. C followed by i, e, y makes s sound
   C followed by a, o, u makes k sound
6. G followed by i, e, y makes j sound
   G followed by a, o, u makes guh sound
7. Silent letters in kn, wr, gn

B. Knows skills of:
1. Forming plurals
   by adding s, es, ies
   by changing f to v and adding es
2. Similarities of sound such as x and cks (box—blocks)
3. Can read Roman numerals I, V, X

C. Syllabication rules
1. There are usually as many syllables in a word as there are vowels
2. Where there is a single consonant between two vowels, the vowel goes with the first syllable (pu/pil)
3. When there is a double consonant, the syllable break is between the two consonants and one is silent (example: lit/tle)

D. Can hyphenate words using syllable rules
E. Understands use of primary accent mark
F. Knows to accent first syllable, unless it is a prefix, otherwise accent second syllable

III. Comprehension:

A. Can find main idea in story
B. Can keep events in proper sequence
C. Can draw logical conclusions
D. Is able to see relationships
E. Can predict outcomes
F. Can follow printed directions
G. Can read for a definite purpose:
1. for pleasure
2. to obtain answer to question
3. to obtain general idea of content

H. Classify items
I. Use index
J. Alphabetize words by first two letters
K. Knows technique of skimming
L. Can determine what source to obtain information (dictionary, encyclopedia, index, glossary, etc.)
M. Use maps and charts

IV. Oral and Silent Reading:

A. Oral Reading
1. Reads with expression
2. Comprehends material read aloud

B. Silent Reading
1. Reads silently without finger pointing, lip movements
2. Comprehends material read silently
3. Reads faster silently than orally

C. Listening
1. Comprehends material read aloud by another
2. Can follow directions read aloud

Group Summary Profile—Third Level

The following pages present a Group Summary Profile at the Third Level which you can use to record the progress of the entire class in mastering the specific reading skills at that level. This profile can assist you in identifying groups of students who need instruction in a particular skill as well as in assessing the strengths and achievement levels of individual students. The Group Profile may also be used in conferences with administrators to discuss the status of a particular class.

Name of Teacher: ______________________________

GROUP SUMMARY PROFILE THIRD LEVEL

Student Names	I. Vocabulary	A. Recognizes Dolch 220 Basic Sight Words	B. Word Meaning	1. Comprehends and uses correctly the following words:	Function Words	Forms of Address	Action Words	Direction Words	Metric Words	Color Words	Career Words	Curriculum Words	II. Word Analysis	A. Refine phonics skills	1. All initial consonant sounds	2. Short and long vowel sounds	3. Changes in words	4. Vowel rules	5. C sound	6. G sound	7. Silent letters in kn, wr, gn	B. Knows skills of	1. Forming plurals	2. Similarities of sound such as x and cks	3. Can read Roman numerals I, V, X	C. Syllabication rules	1. There are usually as many syllables in a word as there are vowels

School: ____________________ Year: __________

2. Where there is a single consonant between two vowels, the vowel goes with the first syllable
3. When there is a double consonant, the syllable break is between the two consonants and one is silent

D. Can hyphenate words using syllable rules

E. Understands use of primary accent mark

F. Knows to accent first syllable, unless it is a prefix, otherwise accent second syllable

III. Comprehension

A. Can find main idea in story

B. Can keep events in proper sequence

C. Can draw logical conclusions

D. Is able to see relationships

E. Can predict outcomes

F. Can follow printed directions

G. Can read for a definite purpose

1. for pleasure
2. to obtain answer to question
3. to obtain general idea of content

H. Classify items

I. Use index

J. Alphabetize words by first two letters

K. Knows technique of skimming

L. Can determine what source to obtain information

M. Use maps and charts

IV. Oral and Silent Reading:

A. Oral Reading

1. Reads with expression
2. Comprehends material read aloud

B. Silent Reading

1. Reads silently without finger pointing, lip movements
2. Comprehends material read silently
3. Reads faster silently than orally

C. Listening

1. Comprehends material read aloud by another
2. Can follow directions read aloud

Reading Skills Competency Tests
Third Level

by Wiley C. Thornton, M. Ed.

The test items which follow are written to measure the reading skills on the "Barbe Reading Skills Check List—Third Level."

The Competency Tests and Check List provide for:

- a quick, informal assessment of a student's competence in reading skills
- diagnosis and prescription of specific reading skill weaknesses and needs
- devising of appropriate teaching strategies for individuals and small or large groups
- continuous evaluation of each student's progress in the basic reading skills
- flexibility in planning the reading instructional program
- immediate feedback to the student and the teacher

The tests are designed to give you an efficient, systematic means to identify the specific reading skills needs of students.

THIRD LEVEL

I. VOCABULARY A. Word Recognition 1. Dolch Basic Sight Words

OBJECTIVE: The student will recognize the 220 Dolch Basic Sight Words by the end of the year.

DIRECTIONS: Part I

Option 1 Have the student say the words to the teacher or aide, noting on the student response sheet those words with which difficulty is encountered.

Option 2 Using flashcards, have the student say the words. Repeat the activity periodically until all the words have been mastered.

____ a
____ about
____ after
____ again
____ all
____ always
____ am
____ an
____ and
____ any
____ are
____ around
____ as
____ ask
____ at
____ ate
____ away
____ be
____ because
____ been
____ before
____ best
____ better
____ big
____ black
____ blue
____ both
____ bring
____ brown
____ but
____ buy
____ by
____ call
____ came
____ can
____ carry
____ clean
____ cold
____ come
____ could
____ cut
____ did
____ do
____ does

MASTERY REQUIREMENT: Recognition of all words by the end of the school year. (See additional words on pages 22, 24, 26, and 28.)

Indicate mastery on the student response sheet with a check.

THIRD LEVEL

I. VOCABULARY

A. Word Recognition

1. Dolch Basic Sight Words

Name ______________________________

Date ______________________________

Mastery ___________

PART I

_____ a

_____ about

_____ after

_____ again

_____ all

_____ always

_____ am

_____ an

_____ and

_____ any

_____ are

_____ around

_____ as

_____ ask

_____ at

_____ ate

_____ away

_____ be

_____ because

_____ been

_____ before

_____ best

_____ better

_____ big

_____ black

_____ blue

_____ both

_____ bring

_____ brown

_____ but

_____ buy

_____ by

_____ call

_____ came

_____ can

_____ carry

_____ clean

_____ cold

_____ come

_____ could

_____ cut

_____ did

_____ do

_____ does

THIRD LEVEL

I. VOCABULARY A. Word Recognition 1. Dolch Basic Sight Words

OBJECTIVE: The student will recognize the 220 Dolch Basic Sight Words by the end of the year.

DIRECTIONS: Part II

Option 1 Have the student say the words to the teacher or aide, noting on the student response sheet those words with which difficulty is encountered.

Option 2 Using flashcards, have the student say the words. Repeat the activity periodically until all the words have been mastered.

____	done	____	for	____	grow
____	don't	____	found	____	had
____	down	____	four	____	has
____	draw	____	from	____	have
____	drink	____	full	____	he
____	eat	____	funny	____	help
____	eight	____	gave	____	her
____	every	____	get	____	here
____	fall	____	give	____	him
____	far	____	go	____	his
____	fast	____	goes	____	hold
____	find	____	going	____	hot
____	first	____	good	____	how
____	five	____	got	____	hurt
____	fly	____	green		

MASTERY REQUIREMENT: Recognition of all words by the end of the school year. (See additional words on pages 20, 24, 26, and 28.)

Indicate mastery on the student response sheet with a check.

THIRD LEVEL

I. VOCABULARY

A. Word Recognition

1. Dolch Basic Sight Words

Name ______________________

Date ______________________

PART II

Mastery __________

____	done	____	for	____	grow
____	don't	____	found	____	had
____	down	____	four	____	has
____	draw	____	from	____	have
____	drink	____	full	____	he
____	eat	____	funny	____	help
____	eight	____	gave	____	her
____	every	____	get	____	here
____	fall	____	give	____	him
____	far	____	go	____	his
____	fast	____	goes	____	hold
____	find	____	going	____	hot
____	first	____	good	____	how
____	five	____	got	____	hurt
____	fly	____	green		

THIRD LEVEL

I. VOCABULARY A. Word Recognition 1. Dolch Basic Sight Words

OBJECTIVE: The student will recognize the 220 Dolch Basic Sight Words by the end of the year.

DIRECTIONS: Part III

Option 1 Have the student say the words to the teacher or aide, noting on the student response sheet those words with which difficulty is encountered.

Option 2 Using flashcards, have the student say the words. Repeat the activity periodically until all the words have been mastered.

____	I	____	like	____	new
____	if	____	little	____	no
____	in	____	live	____	not
____	into	____	long	____	now
____	is	____	look	____	of
____	it	____	made	____	off
____	its	____	make	____	old
____	jump	____	many	____	on
____	just	____	may	____	once
____	keep	____	me	____	one
____	kind	____	much	____	only
____	know	____	must	____	open
____	laugh	____	my	____	or
____	let	____	myself	____	our
____	light	____	never		

MASTERY REQUIREMENT: Recognition of all words by the end of the school year. (See additional words on pages 20, 22, 26, and 28.

Indicate mastery on the student response sheet with a check.

THIRD LEVEL

I. VOCABULARY

A. Word Recognition

1. Dolch Basic Sight Words

Name ______________________

Date ______________________

Mastery __________

PART III

____	I	____	like	____	new
____	if	____	little	____	no
____	in	____	live	____	not
____	into	____	long	____	now
____	is	____	look	____	of
____	it	____	made	____	off
____	its	____	make	____	old
____	jump	____	many	____	on
____	just	____	may	____	once
____	keep	____	me	____	one
____	kind	____	much	____	only
____	know	____	must	____	open
____	laugh	____	my	____	or
____	let	____	myself	____	our
____	light	____	never		

THIRD LEVEL

I. VOCABULARY A. Word Recognition 1. Dolch Basic Sight Words

OBJECTIVE: The student will recognize the 220 Dolch Basic Sight Words by the end of the year.

DIRECTIONS: Part IV

Option 1 Have the student say the words to the teacher or aide, noting on the student response sheet those words with which difficulty is encountered.

Option 2 Using flashcards, have the student say the words. Repeat the activity periodically until all the words have been mastered.

____	out	____	run	____	some
____	over	____	said	____	soon
____	own	____	saw	____	start
____	pick	____	say	____	stop
____	play	____	see	____	take
____	please	____	seven	____	tell
____	pretty	____	shall	____	ten
____	pull	____	she	____	thank
____	put	____	show	____	that
____	ran	____	sing	____	the
____	read	____	sit	____	their
____	red	____	six	____	them
____	ride	____	sleep	____	then
____	right	____	small	____	there
____	round	____	so		

MASTERY REQUIREMENT: Recognition of all words by the end of the school year. (See additional words on pages 20, 22, 24, and 28.)

Indicate mastery on the student response sheet with a check.

THIRD LEVEL

I. VOCABULARY

A. Word Recognition

1. Dolch Basic Sight Words

Name ______________________________

Date ______________________________

Mastery ___________

PART IV

_____ out

_____ over

_____ own

_____ pick

_____ play

_____ please

_____ pretty

_____ pull

_____ put

_____ ran

_____ read

_____ red

_____ ride

_____ right

_____ round

_____ run

_____ said

_____ saw

_____ say

_____ see

_____ seven

_____ shall

_____ she

_____ show

_____ sing

_____ sit

_____ six

_____ sleep

_____ small

_____ so

_____ some

_____ soon

_____ start

_____ stop

_____ take

_____ tell

_____ ten

_____ thank

_____ that

_____ the

_____ their

_____ them

_____ then

_____ there

THIRD LEVEL

I. VOCABULARY A. Word Recognition 1. Dolch Basic Sight Words

OBJECTIVE: The student will recognize the 220 Dolch Basic Sight Words by the end of the year.

DIRECTIONS: Part V

Option 1 Have the student say the words to the teacher or aide, noting on the student response sheet those words with which difficulty is encountered.

Option 2 Using flashcards, have the student say the words. Repeat the activity periodically until all the words have been mastered.

____ these	____ us	____ which
____ they	____ use	____ white
____ think	____ very	____ who
____ this	____ walk	____ why
____ those	____ want	____ will
____ three	____ warm	____ wish
____ to	____ was	____ with
____ today	____ wash	____ work
____ together	____ we	____ would
____ too	____ well	____ write
____ try	____ went	____ yellow
____ two	____ were	____ yes
____ under	____ what	____ you
____ up	____ when	____ your
____ upon	____ where	

MASTERY REQUIREMENT: Recognition of all words by the end of the school year. (See additional words on pages 20, 22, 24, and 26.)

Indicate mastery on the student response sheet with a check.

THIRD LEVEL

I. VOCABULARY

A. Word Recognition

1. Dolch Basic Sight Words

Name ______________________

Date ______________________

Mastery __________

PART V

____	these	____	us	____	which
____	they	____	use	____	white
____	think	____	very	____	who
____	this	____	walk	____	why
____	those	____	want	____	will
____	three	____	warm	____	wish
____	to	____	was	____	with
____	today	____	wash	____	work
____	together	____	we	____	would
____	too	____	well	____	write
____	try	____	went	____	yellow
____	two	____	were	____	yes
____	under	____	what	____	you
____	up	____	when	____	your
____	upon	____	where		

THIRD LEVEL

I. VOCABULARY B. Word Meaning 1. Comprehension and use of words

a. Function words

OBJECTIVE: The student will be able to comprehend and use "function" words.

DIRECTIONS: From the list of words above each of the following sentences, select the word that will best fill the blank in each sentence.

also each most since

1. On our trip, Mother did some of the driving, but Dad drove __most__ of the way.
2. Jenny has not had a sore throat __since__ she had her tonsils out.
3. If Alice and Richard go, Doris may go __also__.
4. There was one present for __each__ person in the family.

against end same while

5. We cleared the middle of the room by pushing our desks back __against__ the wall.
6. Although both of their birthdays are August 5, they were not born the __same__ year.
7. Mother waited in the car __while__ I went to buy the tickets.
8. If he misses a turn, he will have to go to the __end__ of the line.

during more other should thought

9. There are times that we __should__ do things that we do not want to do.
10. Jan's team won __more__ games than anyone else.
11. I did better on that science test than I __thought__ I would.
12. Did it rain __during__ the night?
13. Peggy is Don's __other__ sister.

enough men through women

14. Do you have __enough__ money for a drink and a sandwich?
15. Boys grow up to be __men__.
16. Girls grow up to be __women__.
17. Are you __through__ reading that book?

being such than though

18. Jimmy is oldest, so he had more work to do __than__ anyone else.
19. Seeing the game on TV is fun, but not as good as really __being__ there.
20. Mother will try to go, __though__ she does not have much time.
21. Is there __such__ a word as "sporky?"

MASTERY REQUIREMENT: 17 correct responses

Indicate mastery on the student response sheet with a check.

THIRD LEVEL

I. VOCABULARY

B. Word Meaning

1. Comprehension and use of words

a. Function words

Name ____________________

Date ____________________

Mastery __________

DIRECTIONS: From the list of words above each of the following groups of sentences, select the word that will best fill the blank in each sentence.

also　　each　　most　　since

1. On our trip, Mother did some of the driving, but Dad drove ________ of the way.
2. Jenny has not had a sore throat ________ she had her tonsils out.
3. If Alice and Richard go, Doris may go ________.
4. There was one present for ________ person in the family.

against　　end　　same　　while

5. We cleared the middle of the room by pushing our desks back ________ the wall.
6. Although both of their birthdays are August 5, they were not born the ________ year.
7. Mother waited in the car ________ I went to buy the tickets.
8. If he misses a turn, he will have to go to the ________ of the line.

during　　more　　other　　should　　thought

9. There are times that we ________ do things that we do not want to do.
10. Jan's team won ________ games than anyone else.
11. I did better on that science test than I ________ I would.
12. Did it rain ________ the night?
13. Peggy is Don's ________ sister.

enough　　men　　through　　women

14. Do you have ________ money for a drink and a sandwich?
15. Boys grow up to be ________.
16. Girls grow up to be ________.
17. Are you ________ reading that book?

being　　such　　than　　though

18. Jimmy is oldest, so he had more work to do ________ anyone else.
19. Seeing the game on TV is fun, but not as good as really ________ there.
20. Mother will try to go, ________ she does not have much time.
21. Is there ________ a word as "sporky?"

THIRD LEVEL

I. VOCABULARY B. Word Meaning 1. Comprehension and use of words

b. Direction words

OBJECTIVE: The student will be able to comprehend and use "direction" words.

DIRECTIONS: From the list of words above each of the following groups of sentences, select the word that will best fill the blank in each sentence.

around left toward

1. Susan is helping her father build a fence __around__ their garden.

2. Johnny tripped as he ran __toward__ the goal line.

3. Move the post just a bit to the __left__ and it will be in line.

backward forward right

4. On a ramp, east is to the __right__.

5. To move ahead means to go __forward__.

6. There was no room for Dick to turn around in the tunnel, so he had to crawl out __backward__.

MASTERY REQUIREMENT: All correct

Indicate mastery on the student response sheet with a check.

THIRD LEVEL

I. VOCABULARY

B. Word Meaning

1. Comprehension and use of words

b. Direction words

Name ______________________

Date ______________________

Mastery __________

DIRECTIONS: From the list of words above each of the following groups of sentences, select the word that will best fill the blank in each sentence.

around left toward

1. Susan is helping her father build a fence ______________ their garden.

2. Johnny tripped as he ran ______________ the goal line.

3. Move the post just a bit to the ______________ and it will be in line.

backward forward right

4. On a map, east is to the ______________.

5. To move ahead means to go ______________.

6. There was no room for Dick to turn around in the tunnel, so he had to crawl out ______________.

THIRD LEVEL

I. VOCABULARY B. Word Meaning 1. Comprehension and use of words

c. Action words

OBJECTIVE: The student will be able to comprehend and use "action" words.

DIRECTIONS: From the list of words above each of the following groups of sentences, select the word that will best fill the blank in each sentence.

carry kick skate think

1. Please be quiet while I __think__ about this math problem.

2. Help me __carry__ this post out to the barn.

3. If you get behind that spotted pony, he will __kick__ you.

4. Which is the easiest way to __skate__, roller or ice?

draw push swim throw travel

5. Can you __swim__ the length of the pool?

6. How far can you __throw__ a softball?

7. During the summer we are planning to __travel__ to several places we have never been before.

8. I would like to __draw__ a picture of that old house and barn.

9. We ran out of gas and had to __push__ the car to the side of the road.

MASTERY REQUIREMENT: All correct

Indicate mastery on the student response sheet with a check.

THIRD LEVEL

I. VOCABULARY

B. Word Meaning

1. Comprehension and use of words

c. Action words

Name ______________________________

Date ______________________________

Mastery ___________

DIRECTIONS: From the list of words above each of the following groups of sentences, select the word which will best fill the blank in each sentence.

carry kick skate think

1. Please be quiet while I _____________ about this math problem.

2. Help me _____________ this post out to the barn.

3. If you get behind that spotted pony, he will _____________ you.

4. Which is the easiest way to _____________, roller or ice?

draw push swim throw travel

5. Can you _____________ the length of the pool?

6. How far can you _____________ a softball?

7. During the summer we are planning to _____________ to several places we have never been before.

8. I would like to _____________ a picture of that old house and barn.

9. We ran out of gas and had to _____________ the car to the side of the road.

THIRD LEVEL

I. VOCABULARY **B. Word Meaning** **1. Comprehension and use of words**

d. Forms of address

OBJECTIVE: The student will be able to comprehend and use forms of address.

PART I:

DIRECTIONS: Match the following by writing the proper letter in the blank.

c	1.	Miss	a.	Form of address for a man
a	2.	Mr.	b.	Form of address for a married lady
b	3.	Mrs.	c.	Form of address for an unmarried lady
d	4.	Ms.	d.	Form of address which may be used for a married or unmarried lady

PART II:

DIRECTIONS: Write the correct form of address on the blank line for each of the following.

1. Mr. Smith is a baker. He is my friend.
2. Miss Jones is planning to get married. She has already set the date.
3. When she gets married, her title will change from Miss to Mrs. .
4. My neighbor, Mr. John Lewis, has just won the election.
5. When in doubt whether a lady is married or unmarried, one should use the title Ms. .
6. My teacher's title is ________.

MASTERY REQUIREMENT: 8 correct responses

Indicate mastery on the student response sheet with a check.

THIRD LEVEL

I. VOCABULARY

B. Word Meaning

1. Comprehension and use of words

d. Forms of address

Name ____________________

Date ____________________

Mastery ________

PART I:

DIRECTIONS: Match the following by writing the proper letter in the blank.

____ 1.	Miss	a.	Form of address for a man
____ 2.	Mr.	b.	Form of address for a married lady
____ 3.	Mrs.	c.	Form of address for an unmarried lady
____ 4.	Ms.	d.	Form of address which may be used for a married or unmarried lady

PART II:

DIRECTIONS: Write the correct form of address on the blank line for each of the following.

1. ________ Smith is a baker. He is my friend.

2. ________ Jones is planning to get married. She has already set the date.

3. When she gets married, her title will change from Miss to ________.

4. My neighbor, ________ John Lewis, has just won the election.

5. When in doubt whether a lady is married or unmarried, one should use the title ________.

6. My teacher's title is ________.

THIRD LEVEL

I. VOCABULARY B. Word Meaning 1. Comprehension and use of words

e. Career words

OBJECTIVE: The student will comprehend and use "career" words correctly.

PART I:

DIRECTIONS: Match the words in Column 1 with the right meanings in Column 2.

		Column 1		*Column 2*
c	1.	artist	a.	A place where manufacturing is done
a	2.	factory	b.	Can be exchanged for things which are wanted or needed
b	3.	money	c.	One who produces objects of beauty
e	4.	teacher	d.	The preparing of someone for work of a certain kind
d	5.	training	e.	One who instructs

PART II:

DIRECTIONS: Match the words in Column 1 with the right meanings in Column 2.

		Column 1		*Column 2*
e	1.	lawyer	a.	One who works with doctors or in hospitals to help sick people
d	2.	mechanic	b.	A person's work or job
a	3.	nurse	c.	A place where business is done
c	4.	office	d.	One who repairs things
f	5.	operator	e.	One who helps people with legal problems
b	6.	vocation	f.	One who causes an object or tool to perform work

MASTERY REQUIREMENT: 9 correct responses

Indicate mastery on the student response sheet with a check.

THIRD LEVEL

I. VOCABULARY

B. Word Meaning

1. Comprehension and use of words

e. Career words

Name ______________________

Date ______________________

Mastery __________

PART I:

DIRECTIONS: Match the words in Column 1 with the right meanings in Column 2.

		Column 1		*Column 2*
_____	1.	artist	a.	A place where manufacturing is done
_____	2.	factory	b.	Can be exchanged for things which are wanted or needed
_____	3.	money	c.	One who produces objects of beauty
_____	4.	teacher	d.	The preparing of someone for work of a certain kind
_____	5.	training	e.	One who instructs

PART II:

DIRECTIONS: Match the words in Column 1 with the right meanings in Column 2.

		Column 1		*Column 2*
_____	1.	lawyer	a.	One who works with doctors or in hospitals to help sick people
_____	2.	mechanic	b.	A person's work or job
_____	3.	nurse	c.	A place where business is done
_____	4.	office	d.	One who repairs things
_____	5.	operator	e.	One who helps people with legal problems
_____	6.	vocation	f.	One who causes an object or tool to perform work

THIRD LEVEL

I. VOCABULARY B. Word Meaning 1. Comprehension and use of words
f. Color words

OBJECTIVE: The student will comprehend and use "color" words correctly.

DIRECTIONS: Select one of the words from the following list to fill the blank in each of the sentences.

brown green orange purple

1. Tame rabbits are often white or gray, but wild rabbits are nearly always ___brown___.
2. We could tell he was the king because he was wearing a ___purple___ robe.
3. A citrus fruit whose name is the same as its color is the ___orange___.
4. During the summer, the leaves and grass are ___green___.
5. Most fur coats are the color ___brown___.
6. ___Orange___ pumpkins grew in the farmer's garden.
7. On Saint Patrick's Day many people wear the color ___green___.
8. When the grass dies in the fall, it turns ___brown___.
9. The color word that is divided into syllables between two consonants is ___purple___.
10. The Christmas colors are red and ___green___.

MASTERY REQUIREMENT: 8 correct responses

Indicate mastery on the student response sheet with a check.

THIRD LEVEL

I. VOCABULARY

B. Word Meaning

1. Comprehension and use of words

f. Color words

Name ______________________

Date ______________________

Mastery __________

DIRECTIONS: Select one of the words from the following list to fill the blank in each of the sentences.

brown green orange purple

1. Tame rabbits are often white or gray, but wild rabbits are nearly always ______________.

2. We could tell he was the king because he was wearing a ______________ robe.

3. A citrus fruit whose name is the same as its color is the ______________.

4. During the summer, the leaves and grass are ______________.

5. Most fur coats are the color ______________.

6. ______________ pumpkins grew in the farmer's garden.

7. On Saint Patrick's Day many people wear the color ______________.

8. When the grass dies in the fall, it turns ______________.

9. The color word that is divided into syllables between two consonants is ______________.

10. The Christmas colors are red and ______________.

THIRD LEVEL

I. VOCABULARY   B. Word Meaning   1. Comprehension and use of words

g. Metric words

OBJECTIVE: The students will comprehend and use "metric" words correctly.

PART I:

DIRECTIONS: Match the following by writing the correct letter in the blank.

c	1.	Centigrade	a.	Metric measure of weight
a	2.	Gram	b.	Metric measure of length
d	3.	Liter	c.	A measure of temperature
b	4.	Meter	d.	Metric measure of volume

PART II:

DIRECTIONS: Fill in the correct metric word for each of the following sentences.

centigrade   gram   liter   meter

1. Today it is 25° ___centigrade___.
2. A ___meter___ of ribbon is longer than a yard of ribbon.
3. Some radio stations give both Fahrenheit and ___centigrade___ temperature readings.
4. In England, milk is sold by the ___liter___.
5. Miles are measured by ___meters___.
6. Meat is weighed by the ___gram___ in most countries.

MASTERY REQUIREMENT: 8 correct responses

Indicate mastery on the student response sheet with a check.

THIRD LEVEL

I. VOCABULARY

B. Word Meaning

1. Comprehension and use of words

g. Metric words

Name ______________________

Date ______________________

Mastery __________

PART I:

DIRECTIONS: Match the following by writing the correct letter in the blank.

_____	1. Centigrade		a.	Metric measure of weight
_____	2. Gram		b.	Metric measure of length
_____	3. Liter		c.	A measure of temperature
_____	4. Meter		d.	Metric measure of volume

PART II:

DIRECTIONS: Fill in the correct metric word for each of the following sentences.

centigrade gram liter meter

1. Today it is 25° ____________________.
2. A ____________________ of ribbon is longer than a yard of ribbon.
3. Some radio stations give both Fahrenheit and ____________________ temperature readings.
4. In England, milk is sold by the ____________________.
5. Miles are measured by ____________________.
6. Meat is weighed by the ____________________ in most countries.

THIRD LEVEL

I. VOCABULARY B. Word Meaning 1. Comprehension and use of words

h. Curriculum words

OBJECTIVE: The student will comprehend and use "curriculum" words correctly.

DIRECTIONS: Match the definition with the word by writing the correct letter on the blank line to the left.

d	1.	add	a.	A group of similar things
j	2.	ecology	b.	Not many
f	3.	even	c.	Not as many
b	4.	few	d.	Obtain a sum
k	5.	greater	e.	An emptiness or open place
c	6.	less	f.	Can be grouped by two
i	7.	number	g.	Cannot be grouped by two
g	8.	odd	h.	Obtain a difference
a	9.	set	i.	A unit we count by
e	10.	space	j.	The study of the way man and nature live together
h	11.	subtract	k.	More than or larger than

MASTERY REQUIREMENT: 9 correct responses (See additional words on page 46.)

Indicate mastery on student response sheet with a check.

THIRD LEVEL

I. VOCABULARY

B. Word Meaning

1. Comprehension and use of words

h. Curriculum words

Name ______________________

Date ______________________

Mastery __________

DIRECTIONS: Match the definition with the word by writing the correct letter on the blank line to the left.

____	1. add		a.	A group of similar things
____	2. ecology		b.	Not many
____	3. even		c.	Not as many
____	4. few		d.	Obtain a sum
____	5. greater		e.	An emptiness or open place
____	6. less		f.	Can be grouped by two
____	7. number		g.	Cannot be grouped by two
____	8. odd		h.	Obtain a difference
____	9. set		i.	A unit we count by
____	10. space		j.	The study of the way man and nature live together
____	11. subtract		k.	More than or larger than

THIRD LEVEL

I. VOCABULARY B. Word Meaning 1. Comprehension and use of words
h. Curriculum words

OBJECTIVE: The student will comprehend and use "curriculum" words correctly.

DIRECTIONS: Match the definition with the word by writing the correct letter on the blank line next to each word.

g	1.	American	a.	The four parts of the year
c	2.	country	b.	The earth and everything on it
d	3.	fall	c.	A section of land and population of people under one government
a	4.	seasons	d.	Also known as autumn
j	5.	spring	e.	The country we live in
f	6.	state	f.	One of the fifty parts of our country
i	7.	summer	g.	A person who lives in our country
e	8.	United States	h.	The coldest part of the year
h	9.	winter	i.	The hottest part of the year
b	10.	world	j.	Between winter and summer

MASTERY REQUIREMENT: 9 correct responses (See additional words on page 44.)

Indicate mastery on the student response sheet with a check.

THIRD LEVEL

I. VOCABULARY

B. Word Meaning

1. Comprehension and use of words

h. Curriculum words

Name ______________________

Date ______________________

Mastery __________

DIRECTIONS: Match the definition with the word by writing the correct letter on the blank line next to each word.

_____	1.	American	a.	The four parts of the year
_____	2.	country	b.	The earth and everything on it
_____	3.	fall	c.	A section of land and population of people under one government
_____	4.	seasons	d.	Also known as autumn
_____	5.	spring	e.	The country we live in
_____	6.	state	f.	One of the fifty parts of our country
_____	7.	summer	g.	A person who lives in our country
_____	8.	United States	h.	The coldest part of the year
_____	9.	winter	i.	The hottest part of the year
_____	10.	world	j.	Between winter and summer

THIRD LEVEL

II. WORD ANALYSIS   A. Refine Phonics Skills   1. Initial consonant sounds

OBJECTIVE: The student will know all initial consonant sounds.

DIRECTIONS: Below are two groups of words. In each group, match each word with its beginning sound.

GROUP ONE

1.	does	8	z
2.	fire	3	s
3.	some	5	j
4.	well	1	d
5.	just	4	w
6.	ring	2	f
7.	tiny	7	t
8.	zero	9	n
9.	never	6	r

GROUP TWO

1.	best	4	l
2.	here	9	y
3.	kind	2	h
4.	like	6	p
5.	mean	1	b
6.	penny	5	m
7.	quiet	8	v
8.	very	7	q
9.	yellow	3	k

MASTERY REQUIREMENT: 15 correct responses (See additional sounds on page 50.)

Indicate mastery on the student response sheet with a check.

THIRD LEVEL

II. WORD ANALYSIS

A. Refine Phonics Skills

1. Initial consonant sounds

Name ______________________

Date ______________________

Mastery __________

DIRECTIONS: Below are two groups of words. In each group, match each word with its beginning sound.

GROUP ONE

1.	does	____	z
2.	fire	____	s
3.	some	____	j
4.	well	____	d
5.	just	____	w
6.	ring	____	f
7.	tiny	____	t
8.	zero	____	n
9.	never	____	r

GROUP TWO

1.	best	____	l
2.	here	____	y
3.	kind	____	h
4.	like	____	p
5.	mean	____	b
6.	penny	____	m
7.	quiet	____	v
8.	very	____	q
9.	yellow	____	k

THIRD LEVEL

II. WORD ACTIVITIES A. Refine Phonics Skills 1. Initial consonant sounds

OBJECTIVE: The student will know all initial consonant sounds.

DIRECTIONS: Below are three groups of words. In each group, match each word with its beginning sound.

GROUP ONE

1.	bring	9	bl
2.	cream	5	th
3.	swing	2	cr
4.	shine	4	sh
5.	third	8	wh
6.	chair	11	cl
7.	smile	1	br
8.	white	10	gl
9.	blue	7	sm
10.	glass	6	ch
11.	close	3	sw

GROUP TWO

1.	please	6	sn
2.	green	10	fl
3.	scare	8	dr
4.	from	5	pr
5.	pretty	9	st
6.	snail	2	gr
7.	travel	3	sc
8.	drain	1	pl
9.	stamp	7	tr
10.	flower	4	fr

GROUP THREE

1.	scream	3	chr
2.	string	6	thr
3.	Christmas	1	scr
4.	school	4	sch
5.	spring	2	str
6.	throw	5	spr

MASTERY REQUIREMENT: 23 correct responses (See additional sounds on page 48.)

Indicate mastery on the student response sheet with a check.

THIRD LEVEL

II. WORD ANALYSIS

A. Refine Phonics Skills

1. Initial consonant sounds

Name ______________________

Date ______________________

Mastery __________

DIRECTIONS: Below are three groups of words. In each group, match each word with its beginning sound.

GROUP ONE

1.	bring	_____	bl
2.	cream	_____	th
3.	swing	_____	cr
4.	shine	_____	sh
5.	third	_____	wh
6.	chair	_____	cl
7.	smile	_____	br
8.	white	_____	gl
9.	blue	_____	sm
10.	glass	_____	ch
11.	close	_____	sw

GROUP TWO

1.	please	_____	sn
2.	green	_____	fl
3.	scare	_____	dr
4.	from	_____	pr
5.	pretty	_____	st
6.	snail	_____	gr
7.	travel	_____	sc
8.	drain	_____	pl
9.	stamp	_____	tr
10.	flower	_____	fr

GROUP THREE

1.	scream	_____	chr
2.	string	_____	thr
3.	Christmas	_____	scr
4.	school	_____	sch
5.	spring	_____	str
6.	throw	_____	spr

THIRD LEVEL

II. WORD ANALYSIS A. Refine Phonics Skills 2. Short and long vowel sounds

OBJECTIVE: The student will distinguish long and short vowel sounds.

DIRECTIONS: Say each word silently. If the vowel *that you hear* is long, write the word in the column under LONG; if it is short, write the word in the column under SHORT.

	LONG	SHORT
1. tan	________	tan
2. same	same	________
3. please	please	________
4. shed	________	shed
5. spite	spite	________
6. flit	________	flit
7. dog	________	dog
8. bloat	bloat	________
9. gull	________	gull
10. cue	cue	________

MASTERY REQUIREMENT: 9 correct responses

Indicate mastery on the student response sheet with a check.

THIRD LEVEL

II. WORD ANALYSIS

A. Refine Phonics Skills

2. Short and long vowel sounds

Name ______________________________

Date ______________________________

Mastery ___________

DIRECTIONS: Say each word silently. If the vowel *that you hear* is long, write the word in the column under LONG; if it is short, write the word in the column under SHORT.

	LONG	SHORT
1. tan	______________	______________
2. same	______________	______________
3. please	______________	______________
4. shed	______________	______________
5. spite	______________	______________
6. flit	______________	______________
7. dog	______________	______________
8. bloat	______________	______________
9. gull	______________	______________
10. cue	______________	______________

THIRD LEVEL

II. WORD ANALYSIS   A. Refine Phonics Skills   3. Changes in words

a. Adding s, es, d, ed, ing, er, est

OBJECTIVE: The student will change words by adding the proper ending, choosing from s, es, d, ed, ing, er, est.

DIRECTIONS: Fill the blanks in these sentences by placing the proper ending on the word at the end of the sentence. Choose from this list of endings:

s   es   d   ed   ing   er   est

1. How many ___days___ will it be before we have a holiday? ___day___
2. Pete is ___older___ than his sister. ___old___
3. Jan ___goes___ to California every summer. ___go___
4. Sarah is the ___smartest___ girl in the class. ___smart___
5. When will you be through ___building___ that thing? ___build___
6. How long have you ___owed___ me that dime? ___owe___
7. We ___talked___ for a long time yesterday. ___talk___
8. Two ___boxes___ fell off the back of the truck. ___box___
9. Frank is ___working___ in a grocery store on Saturdays. ___work___
10. It has ___rained___ only two times this month. ___rain___
11. She is the ___fastest___ swimmer on the team. ___fast___
12. The tug ___whistled___ as it chugged up the river. ___whistle___

MASTERY REQUIREMENT: 9 correct responses

Indicate mastery on the student response sheet with a check.

THIRD LEVEL

II. WORD ANALYSIS

A. Refine Phonics Skills

3. Changes in words

a. Adding e, es, d, ed, ing, er, est

Name ____________________

Date ____________________

Mastery__________

DIRECTIONS: Fill the blanks in these sentences by placing the proper ending on the word at the end of the sentence. Choose from this list of endings:

s   es   d   ed   ing   er   est

1.	How many ____________ will it be before we have a holiday?	day
2.	Pete is ____________ than his sister.	old
3.	Jan ____________ to California every summer.	go
4.	Sarah is the ____________ girl in the class.	smart
5.	When will you be through ____________ that thing?	build
6.	How long have you ____________ me that dime?	owe
7.	We ____________ for a long time yesterday.	talk
8.	Two ____________ fell off the back of the truck.	box
9.	Frank is ____________ in a grocery store on Saturdays.	work
10.	It has ____________ only two times this month.	rain
11.	She is the ____________ swimmer on the team.	fast
12.	The tug ____________ as it chugged up the river.	whistle

THIRD LEVEL

II. WORD ANALYSIS **A. Refine Phonics Skills** **3. Changes in words**

b. Dropping e and adding ing

OBJECTIVE: The student will correctly drop the final e in words before adding ing.

DIRECTIONS: Fill the blank in each sentence by using the correct form of the word at the end of the sentence.

1. The sun is __shining__ brightly. __shine__
2. Are you __writing__ a letter to your uncle? __write__
3. May I borrow your hatchet when you are through __using__ it? __use__
4. She fell down the steps as we were __leaving__. __leave__
5. Jack has been __saving__ money for Christmas all year. __save__
6. Look at the cattle __grazing__ in the pasture. __graze__
7. How long has Beth been __serving__ as president? __serve__
8. The cars were __sliding__ on the icy roads. __slide__
9. What are you __giving__ John for his birthday? __give__
10. Ann is __making__ a new toy for her brother. __make__

MASTERY REQUIREMENT: 8 correct responses

Indicate mastery on the student response sheet with a check.

THIRD LEVEL

II. WORD ANALYSIS

A. Refine Phonics Skills

3. Changes in words

b. Dropping e and adding ing

Name ____________________

Date ____________________

Mastery __________

DIRECTIONS: Fill the blank in each sentence by using the correct form of the word at the end of the sentence.

1. The sun is __________ brightly. shine

2. Are you __________ a letter to your uncle? write

3. May I borrow your hatchet when you are through __________ it? use

4. She fell down the steps as we were __________. leave

5. Jack has been __________ money for Christmas all year. save

6. Look at the cattle __________ in the pasture. graze

7. How long has Beth been __________ as president? serve

8. The cars were __________ on the icy roads. slide

9. What are you __________ John for his birthday? give

10. Ann is __________ a new toy for her brother. make

THIRD LEVEL

II. WORD ANALYSIS   A. Refine Phonics Skills   3. Changes in words

c. Doubling consonant before adding ing

OBJECTIVE: The student will correctly double the final consonant in words before adding ing.

DIRECTIONS: Fill the blank in each sentence by using the correct form of the word at the end of the sentence.

1. The __swimming__ pool opens at noon on Sunday. __swim__

2. Mother is outside __digging__ in her flower bed. __dig__

3. Have you been __sitting__ there long? __sit__

4. Stop __grabbing__ my arm! __grab__

5. He missed three spelling words for not __dotting__ an "i." __dot__

6. Sue was the __batting__ champion of her softball league. __bat__

7. Two deer came __running__ across the field. __run__

8. A policeman was __stopping__ all trucks on the highway. __stop__

9. The doorbell rang while I was __putting__ on my coat. __put__

10. I am __shutting__ the gate to keep rabbits out of the garden. __shut__

MASTERY REQUIREMENT: 9 correct responses

Indicate mastery on the student response sheet with a check.

THIRD LEVEL

II. WORD ANALYSIS

A. Refine Phonics Skills

3. Changes in words

c. Doubling consonant before adding ing

Name ____________________

Date ____________________

Mastery __________

DIRECTIONS: Fill the blank in each sentence by using the correct form of the word at the end of the sentence.

1. The ____________ pool opens at noon on Sunday. swim

2. Mother is outside ____________ in her flower bed. dig

3. Have you been ____________ there long? sit

4. Stop ____________ my arm! grab

5. He missed three spelling words for not ____________ an "i." dot

6. Sue was the ____________ champion of her softball league. bat

7. Two deer came ____________ across the field. run

8. A policeman was ____________ all trucks on the highway. stop

9. The doorbell rang while I was ____________ on my coat. put

10. I am ____________ the gate to keep rabbits out of the garden. shut

THIRD LEVEL

II. WORD ANALYSIS   A. Refine Phonics Skills   3. Changes in words

d. Changing y to i before adding es

OBJECTIVE: The student will correctly change y to i before adding es.

DIRECTIONS: Fill the blank in each sentence by using the correct form of the word at the end of the sentence.

1. My kite ___flies___ better than yours does. ___fly___

2. How many ___tries___ do you get for a dime? ___try___

3. I want French ___fries___ with my hamburger. ___fry___

4. He is invited to two ___parties___ on the same day. ___party___

5. There are three large ___factories___ in that part of town. ___factory___

6. Dad was in several ___countries___ while he was in the Air Force. ___country___

7. That truck ___carries___ over a ton of earth. ___carry___

8. His sister will ___marry___ in June. ___marry___

9. Helen and I picked ___berries___ in the garden. ___berry___

10. My dog usually ___buries___ his bones by the back door. ___bury___

11. The baby ___cries___ when he is hungry. ___cry___

12. The hay ___dries___ in the sun after it is cut. ___dry___

MASTERY REQUIREMENT: 9 correct responses

Indicate mastery on the student response sheet with a check.

THIRD LEVEL

II. WORD ANALYSIS

A. Refine Phonics Skills

3. Changes in words

d. Changing y to i before adding es

Name ______________________

Date ______________________

Mastery __________

DIRECTIONS: Fill the blank in each sentence by using the correct form of the word at the end of the sentence.

1. My kite ____________ better than yours does. fly

2. How many ____________ do you get for a dime? try

3. I want French ____________ with my hamburger. fry

4. He is invited to two ____________ on the same day. party

5. There are three large ____________ in that part of town. factory

6. Dad was in several ____________ while he was in the Air Force. country

7. That truck ____________ over a ton of earth. carry

8. His sister will ____________ in June. marry

9. Helen and I picked ____________ in the garden. berry

10. My dog usually ____________ his bones by the back door. bury

11. The baby ____________ when he is hungry. cry

12. The hay ____________ in the sun after it is cut. dry

THIRD LEVEL

II. WORD ANALYSIS A. Refine Phonics Skills 4. Vowel rules

a. Vowel in one-syllable word is short

OBJECTIVE: The student will identify vowels in one-syllable words as being short.

DIRECTIONS: Draw a circle around each word that contains a short vowel.

1. pan (circled)
2. before
3. dip (circled)
4. run (circled)
5. lately
6. pony
7. bet (circled)
8. croak
9. fireplace
10. top (circled)

MASTERY REQUIREMENT: 8 correct responses

Indicate mastery on the student response sheet with a check.

THIRD LEVEL

II. WORD ANALYSIS

A. Refine Phonics Skills

4. Vowel rules

a. Vowel in one-syllable word is short

Name ____________________

Date ____________________

Mastery __________

DIRECTIONS: Draw a circle around each word that contains a short vowel.

1. pan
2. before
3. dip
4. run
5. lately
6. pony
7. bet
8. croak
9. fireplace
10. top

THIRD LEVEL

II. WORD ANALYSIS A. Refine Phonics Skills 4. Vowel rules

b. Vowel in word or syllable ending in e is long

OBJECTIVE: The student will identify vowels in words or syllables ending in e as long.

DIRECTIONS: Draw a circle around each word that contains a long vowel.

1. tape
2. kin
3. behave
4. cute
5. these
6. time
7. tap
8. lot
9. pet
10. put

MASTERY REQUIREMENT: 8 correct responses

Indicate mastery on the student response sheet with a check.

THIRD LEVEL

II. WORD ANALYSIS

A. Refine Phonics Skills

4. Vowel rules

b. Vowel in word or syllable ending in e is long

Name ______________________

Date ______________________

Mastery __________

DIRECTIONS: Draw a circle around each word that contains a long vowel.

1. tape
2. kin
3. behave
4. cute
5. these
6. time
7. tap
8. lot
9. pet
10. put

II. WORD ANALYSIS **A. Refine Phonics Skills** **4. Vowel rules**
c. Two vowels together

OBJECTIVE: The student will know that when two vowels are together, the first is often long and the second is silent.

DIRECTIONS: In the following words, underline the long vowels and draw a circle around the silent vowels.

1. g l e (a) m
2. b e (a) m
3. b o (a) t
4. t a (i) l
5. m a (i) d
6. f o (a) m
7. s t e (a) l
8. c l u (e)
9. s o (a) p
10. h e (a) t

MASTERY REQUIREMENT: 8 correct responses

Indicate mastery on the student response sheet with a check.

THIRD LEVEL

II. WORD ANALYSIS

A. Refine Phonics Skills

4. Vowel rules

c. Two vowels together

Name ______________________

Date ______________________

Mastery __________

DIRECTIONS: In the following words, underline the long vowels and draw a circle around the silent vowels.

1. g l e a m

2. b e a m

3. b o a t

4. t a i l

5. m a i d

6. f o a m

7. s t e a l

8. c l u e

9. s o a p

10. h e a t

THIRD LEVEL

II. WORD ANALYSIS A. Refine Phonics Skills 4. Vowel rules

d. Vowel alone in word

OBJECTIVE: The student will know that a vowel alone in a word is usually short.

DIRECTIONS: Draw a circle around each of the following words that has a short vowel.

1. (man)
2. (pit)
3. mule
4. (let)
5. deed
6. mine
7. pane
8. (mop)
9. (pup)
10. pole

MASTERY REQUIREMENT: 9 correct responses

Indicate mastery on the student response sheet with a check.

THIRD LEVEL

II. WORD ANALYSIS

A. Refine Phonics Skills

4. Vowel rules

d. Vowel alone in word

Name ______________________________

Date ______________________________

Mastery __________

DIRECTIONS: Draw a circle around each of the following words that has a short vowel.

1. man

2. pit

3. mule

4. let

5. deed

6. mine

7. pane

8. mop

9. pup

10. pole

THIRD LEVEL

II. WORD ANALYSIS A. Refine Phonics Skills 5. Sounds of c

OBJECTIVE: The student will differentiate between conditions which cause c to have the s sound and the k sound.

DIRECTIONS: Circle the correct beginning sound for each of the following words. If you think the c would have the s sound, circle the s; if you think the c would make a k sound, circle the k.

1.	cellar	(s)	k
2.	calf	s	(k)
3.	coal	s	(k)
4.	call	s	(k)
5.	cold	s	(k)
6.	certain	(s)	k
7.	coat	s	(k)
8.	ceiling	(s)	k
9.	came	s	(k)
10.	cent	(s)	k
11.	cell	(s)	k
12.	cup	s	(k)

MASTERY REQUIREMENT: 9 correct responses

Indicate mastery on the student response sheet with a check.

THIRD LEVEL

II. WORD ANALYSIS

A. Refine Phonics Skills

5. Sounds of c

Name ____________________

Date ____________________

Mastery __________

DIRECTIONS: Circle the correct beginning sound for each of the following words. If you think the c would have the s sound, circle the s; if you think the c would make a k sound, circle the k.

1.	cellar	s	k
2.	calf	s	k
3.	coal	s	k
4.	call	s	k
5.	cold	s	k
6.	certain	s	k
7.	coat	s	k
8.	ceiling	s	k
9.	came	s	k
10.	cent	s	k
11.	cell	s	k
12.	cup	s	k

THIRD LEVEL

II. WORD ANALYSIS A. Refine Phonics Skills 6. Sounds of g

OBJECTIVE: The student will differentiate between conditions which cause g to have the j sound and the guh sound.

DIRECTIONS: Circle the correct beginning sound for each of the following words. If you think the g would have the j sound, circle the j after the word; if you think the g would have the guh sound, circle the guh after the word.

1.	gem	(j)	guh
2.	game	j	(guh)
3.	gate	j	(guh)
4.	gentle	(j)	guh
5.	goat	j	(guh)
6.	general	(j)	guh
7.	gum	j	(guh)
8.	gift	j	(guh)
9.	germ	(j)	guh
10.	girl	j	(guh)

MASTERY REQUIREMENT: 7 correct responses

Indicate mastery on the student response sheet with a check.

THIRD LEVEL

II. WORD ANALYSIS

A. Refine Phonics Skills

6. Sounds of g

Name ______________________________

Date ______________________________

Mastery __________

DIRECTIONS: Circle the correct beginning sound for each of the following words. If you think the g would have the j sound, circle the j after the word; if you think the g would have the guh sound, circle the guh after the word.

1.	gem	j	guh
2.	game	j	guh
3.	gate	j	guh
4.	gentle	j	guh
5.	goat	j	guh
6.	general	j	guh
7.	gum	j	guh
8.	gift	j	guh
9.	germ	j	guh
10.	girl	j	guh

THIRD LEVEL

II. WORD ANALYSIS A. Refine Phonics Skills 7. Silent letters in kn, wr, gn

OBJECTIVE: The student will know the conditions that cause k, w, and g to be silent as initial letters.

DIRECTIONS: Here are twelve words beginning with consonant blends. Read each of these words to yourself and circle the silent consonant in each word.

1. (k) n o w
2. (w) r i t e
3. (g) n o m e
4. (w) r o n g
5. (k) n o t
6. (w) r e a t h
7. (g) n a w
8. (w) r i n g
9. (k) n o c k
10. (g) n a r l
11. (k) n i t
12. (w) r i s t

MASTERY REQUIREMENT: 9 correct responses

Indicate mastery on the student response sheet with a check.

THIRD LEVEL

II. WORD ANALYSIS

A. Refine Phonics Skills

7. Silent letters in kn, wr, gn

Name ______________________

Date ______________________

Mastery __________

DIRECTIONS: Here are twelve words beginning with consonant blends. Read each of these words to yourself and circle the silent consonant in each word.

1. k n o w

2. w r i t e

3. g n o m e

4. w r o n g

5. k n o t

6. w r e a t h

7. g n a w

8. w r i n g

9. k n o c k

10. g n a r l

11. k n i t

12. w r i s t

THIRD LEVEL

II. WORD ANALYSIS B. Knows Skills 1. Forming plurals

a. Adding, s, es, ies

OBJECTIVE: The student will form plurals correctly by adding s, es, ies.

DIRECTIONS: Write the plural for each of these words.

1.	paper	papers
2.	book	books
3.	torch	torches
4.	rabbit	rabbits
5.	fox	foxes
6.	studio	studios
7.	college	colleges
8.	buzz	buzzes
9.	army	armies
10.	baby	babies
11.	match	matches
12.	puppy	puppies

MASTERY REQUIREMENT: 10 correct responses

Indicate mastery on the student response sheet with a check.

THIRD LEVEL

II. WORD ANALYSIS

B. Knows Skills

1. Forming plurals

a. Adding s, es, ies

Name ____________________

Date ____________________

Mastery __________

DIRECTIONS: Write the plural for each of these words.

1. paper ____________
2. book ____________
3. torch ____________
4. rabbit ____________
5. fox ____________
6. studio ____________
7. college ____________
8. buzz ____________
9. army ____________
10. baby ____________
11. match ____________
12. puppy ____________

THIRD LEVEL

II. WORD ANALYSIS B. Knows Skills 1. Forming plurals

b. Changing f to v and adding es

OBJECTIVE: The student will form plurals correctly by changing f to v and adding es.

DIRECTIONS: Write the plurals for each of these words.

1.	self	selves
2.	wolf	wolves
3.	calf	calves
4.	knife	knives
5.	half	halves
6.	shelf	shelves
7.	wife	wives
8.	leaf	leaves
9.	thief	thieves
10.	scarf	scarves

MASTERY REQUIREMENT: 7 correct responses

Indicate mastery on the student response sheet with a check.

THIRD LEVEL

II. WORD ANALYSIS

B. Knows Skills

1. Forming plurals

b. Changing f to v and adding es

Name ______________________

Date ______________________

Mastery __________

DIRECTIONS: Write the plurals for each of these words.

1. self ______________

2. wolf ______________

3. calf ______________

4. knife ______________

5. half ______________

6. shelf ______________

7. wife ______________

8. leaf ______________

9. thief ______________

10. scarf ______________

THIRD LEVEL

II. WORD ANALYSIS B. Knows Skills 2. Similarities of sounds

OBJECTIVE: The student will know that different letter combinations may make similar sounds.

DIRECTIONS: For each word in the first column, find the word in the second column where the underlined letters make the same sound. Write the letter in the blank.

d	1.	too	a.	curled
f	2.	box	b.	bluffed
a	3.	world	c.	giraffe
e	4.	drowse	d.	blew
b	5.	tuft	e.	plows
c	6.	laugh	f.	blocks

c	1.	tux	a.	toad
f	2.	write	b.	steak
b	3.	ache	c.	trucks
a	4.	explode	d.	winks
d	5.	minx	e.	shown
e	6.	cone	f.	bright

MASTERY REQUIREMENT: 10 correct responses

Indicate mastery on the student response sheet with a check.

THIRD LEVEL

II. WORD ANALYSIS

B. Knows Skills

2. Similarities of sounds

Name ____________________

Date ____________________

Mastery __________

DIRECTIONS: For each word in the first column, find the word in the second column where the underlined letters make the same sound. Write the letter in the blank.

____	1.	too	a.	curled
____	2.	box	b.	bluffed
____	3.	world	c.	giraffe
____	4.	drowse	d.	blew
____	5.	tuft	e.	plows
____	6.	laugh	f.	blocks

____	1.	tux	a.	toad
____	2.	write	b.	steak
____	3.	ache	c.	trucks
____	4.	explode	d.	winks
____	5.	minx	e.	shown
____	6.	cone	f.	bright

THIRD LEVEL

II. WORD ANALYSIS B. Knows Skills 3. Roman numerals

OBJECTIVE: The student will read the Roman numerals I, V, and X.

DIRECTIONS: Match the following by writing the correct letter in the blank.

c	1.	Five	a.	I
a	2.	One	b.	X
b	3.	Ten	c.	V

MASTERY REQUIREMENT: All correct

Indicate mastery on the student response sheet with a check.

THIRD LEVEL

II. WORD ANALYSIS

B. Knows Skills

3. Roman numerals

Name ______________________________

Date ______________________________

Mastery ___________

DIRECTIONS: Match the following by writing the correct letter in the blank.

_____ 1.	Five	a.	I
_____ 2.	One	b.	X
_____ 3.	Ten	c.	V

THIRD LEVEL

II. WORD ANALYSIS C. Syllabication 1. Usually as many syllables in word as there are vowels

OBJECTIVE: The student will know there are usually as many syllables in a word as there are vowels.

DIRECTIONS: How many syllables does each of the following words have? Write the number on the line next to each word.

1. card 1
2. storm 1
3. mushroom 2
4. trash 1
5. zipper 2
6. dream 1
7. airplane 2
8. dinner 2
9. sidewalk 2
10. basketball 3
11. hamburger 3
12. automobile 4

MASTERY REQUIREMENT: 10 correct responses

Indicate mastery on the student response sheet with a check.

THIRD LEVEL

II. WORD ANALYSIS

C. Syllabication

1. Usually as many syllables in word as there are vowels

Name ____________________

Date ____________________

Mastery __________

DIRECTIONS: How many syllables does each of the following words have? Write the number on the line next to each word.

1. card ____
2. storm ____
3. mushroom ____
4. trash ____
5. zipper ____
6. dream ____
7. airplane ____
8. dinner ____
9. sidewalk ____
10. basketball ____
11. hamburger ____
12. automobile ____

THIRD LEVEL

II. WORD ANALYSIS C. Syllabication 2. Single consonant between two vowels

OBJECTIVE: The student will know that when a single consonant comes between two vowels, the vowel goes with the first syllable.

DIRECTIONS: Draw a line (/) in the following words where they should be divided into syllables.

1. p u/p i l
2. m i/n o r
3. l a/t e x
4. s e/r e n e
5. r e/t i r e
6. p a/t e n t
7. c h o/r a l
8. b a/g e l
9. s t o/r y
10. n a/v y
11. p a/p e r
12. c a/b l e

MASTERY REQUIREMENT: 9 correct responses

Indicate mastery on the student response sheet with a check.

THIRD LEVEL

II. WORD ANALYSIS

C. Syllabication

2. Single consonant between two vowels

Name ______________________

Date ______________________

Mastery __________

DIRECTIONS: Draw a line (/) in the following words where they should be divided into syllables.

1. p u p i l

2. m i n o r

3. l a t e x

4. s e r e n e

5. r e t i r e

6. p a t e n t

7. c h o r a l

8. b a g e l

9. s t o r y

10. n a v y

11. p a p e r

12. c a b l e

THIRD LEVEL

II. WORD ANALYSIS   C. Syllabication   3. Double consonants

OBJECTIVE: The student will know that in the case of double consonants, the syllable break comes between the two consonants.

DIRECTIONS: Draw a line (/) in the following words where you think they should be divided into syllables.

1. m i l / l e r

2. l i t / t l e

3. d o l / l y

4. f i d / d l e

5. n i b / b l e

6. a l / l e y

7. c a t / t l e

8. h i t / t e r

9. f l a n / n e l

10. c h a t / t e r

11. p u l / l e y

12. s e t / t l e r

MASTERY REQUIREMENT: 8 correct responses

Indicate mastery on the student response sheet with a check.

THIRD LEVEL

II. WORD ANALYSIS

C. Syllabication

3. Double consonants

Name ____________________

Date ____________________

Mastery __________

DIRECTIONS: Draw a line (/) in the following words where you think they should be divided into syllables.

1. m i l l e r

2. l i t t l e

3. d o l l y

4. f i d d l e

5. n i b b l e

6. a l l e y

7. c a t t l e

8. h i t t e r

9. f l a n n e l

10. c h a t t e r

11. p u l l e y

12. s e t t l e r

THIRD LEVEL

II. WORD ANALYSIS D. Hyphenation of Words

OBJECTIVE: The student will hyphenate words correctly using syllable rules.

DIRECTIONS: Below are ten words. The second column shows each word continued from one line to the next. Some of the words are continued correctly and some are incorrect. Place a (√) by those that are correct and an (X) by those that are incorrect.

1. practical	prac- tical	√
2. simple	sim- ple	√
3. hornet	hor- net	√
4. horrible	hor- rible	√
5. spoon	spo- on	X
6. earring	ear- ring	√
7. apiece	a- piece	X
8. studio	studi- o	X
9. baked	bak- ed	X
10. slight	sli- ght	X

MASTERY REQUIREMENT: 8 correct responses

Indicate mastery on the student response sheet with a check.

THIRD LEVEL

II. WORD ANALYSIS

D. Hyphenation of Words

Name ______________________

Date ______________________

Mastery __________

DIRECTIONS: Below are ten words. The second column shows each word continued from one line to the next. Some of the words are continued correctly and some are incorrect. Place a (√) by those that are correct and an (X) by those that are incorrect.

1.	practical	prac- tical	____
2.	simple	sim- ple	____
3.	hornet	hor- net	____
4.	horrible	hor- rible	____
5.	spoon	spo- on	____
6.	earring	ear- ring	____
7.	apiece	a- piece	____
8.	studio	studi- o	____
9.	baked	bak- ed	____
10.	slight	sli- ght	____

THIRD LEVEL

II. WORD ANALYSIS E. Primary Accent Mark

OBJECTIVE: The student will understand the use of the primary accent mark.

DIRECTIONS: Read the following words and underline the syllable that should receive the accent mark.

1. mu-sic
2. oc-to-pus
3. dis-tance
4. ma-chine
5. veg-e-ta-ble
6. tor-ped-o
7. col-o-ny
8. sta-tion
9. dis-hon-est
10. ham-bur-ger
11. ed-u-ca-tion
12. mil-i-tar-y

MASTERY REQUIREMENT: 9 correct responses

Indicate mastery on the student response sheet with a check.

THIRD LEVEL

II. WORD ANALYSIS

E. Primary Accent Mark

Name ______________________________

Date ______________________________

Mastery __________

DIRECTIONS: Read the following words and underline the syllable that should receive the accent mark.

1. mu-sic

2. oc-to-pus

3. dis-tance

4. ma-chine

5. veg-e-ta-ble

6. tor-ped-o

7. col-o-ny

8. sta-tion

9. dis-hon-est

10. ham-bur-ger

11. ed-u-ca-tion

12. mil-i-tar-y

THIRD LEVEL

II. WORD ANALYSIS F. Accent First Syllable unless Prefix

OBJECTIVE: The student will know that the first syllable usually receives the accent unless it is a prefix.

DIRECTIONS: Underline the syllable which should receive the primary accent in these words.

1. gold-en
2. cot-ton
3. re-port
4. lot-te-ry
5. ho-ly
6. ob-vi-ous
7. skel-e-ton
8. un-ti-dy
9. ag-o-ny
10. be-hind

MASTERY REQUIREMENT: 9 correct responses

Indicate mastery on the student response sheet with a check.

THIRD LEVEL

II. WORD ANALYSIS

F. Accent First Syllable
unless Prefix

Name ______________________

Date ______________________

Mastery __________

DIRECTIONS: Underline the syllable which should receive the primary accent in these words.

1. gold-en

2. cot-ton

3. re-port

4. lot-te-ry

5. ho-ly

6. ob-vi-ous

7. skel-e-ton

8. un-ti-dy

9. ag-o-ny

10. be-hind

THIRD LEVEL

III. COMPREHENSION   A. Main Idea

OBJECTIVE: The student will be able to find the main idea in a story.

DIRECTIONS: Read this story, then answer the question below.

Do you know what a cacao is? A cacao is a large, yellow fruit. This fruit grows quite large—sometimes as much as eight or nine inches long. It is filled with many seeds about the size of large peanuts. These seeds are used to make a kind of candy most children like very much. The tree on which the cacao fruit grows is found in the warm, wet countries of South and Central America. The workers on the farms that grow cacao watch the fruit very closely to know when it is ripe. At just the right time, the seeds are taken out, cleaned, and roasted. After they have roasted just enough, they are mashed into a paste. Sugar and vanilla are added to the paste. The paste is then spread out in thin sheets to dry. After it has hardened enough, it is cut into bars and wrapped. Do you know what it is yet? Right! Chocolate bars!

What is this story about?

____ 1. How to grow a cacao tree

__X__ 2. How a chocolate bar is made

____ 3. Plants that grow in warm countries

____ 4. The kinds of candy that are made from chocolate bars

MASTERY REQUIREMENT: Correct response

Indicate mastery on the student response sheet with a check.

THIRD LEVEL

III. COMPREHENSION

A. Main Idea

Name ______________________

Date ______________________

Mastery __________

DIRECTIONS: Read this story, then answer the question below.

Do you know what a cacao is? A cacao is a large, yellow fruit. This fruit grows quite large–sometimes as much as eight or nine inches long. It is filled with many seeds about the size of large peanuts. These seeds are used to make a kind of candy most children like very much. The tree on which the cacao fruit grows is found in the warm, wet countries of South and Central America. The workers on the farms that grow cacao watch the fruit very closely to know when it is ripe. At just the right time, the seeds are taken out, cleaned, and roasted. After they have roasted just enough, they are mashed into a paste. Sugar and vanilla are added to the paste. The paste is then spread out in thin sheets to dry. After it has hardened enough, it is cut into bars and wrapped. Do you know what it is yet? Right! Chocolate bars!

What is this story about?

____ 1. How to grow a cacao tree

____ 2. How a chocolate bar is made

____ 3. Plants that grow in warm countries

____ 4. The kinds of candy that are made from chocolate bars

THIRD LEVEL

III. COMPREHENSION B. Sequence of Events

OBJECTIVE: The student will keep events in a story in proper sequence.

DIRECTIONS: Read this story, then try to answer the questions below without looking back at the story.

Kay Baker and her dad put in a full day of work on Saturday fencing in the back yard. Then Sunday afternoon they worked until nearly dark building a doghouse. Now Prince had a safe place to play and a dry place to sleep.

Kay found an article in a book about dogs like Prince. He was a German Shepherd. They make good playmates for children, but are also excellent watchdogs and fighters when they need to be.

Prince is small now because he is just a puppy. He can almost crawl through the fence. When he grows up, though, he will be a large dog. Some German Shepherds weigh as much as a hundred pounds. He will be a good pet and also a useful and brave watchdog.

1. When did the Baker family get Prince?

____ a. When they saw how he could fight.

____ b. When he was grown.

__X__ c. When he was little.

2. The first night Prince could sleep in his new doghouse was

____ a. Saturday.

__X__ b. Sunday.

3. According to the story, Kay and her dad finished working

____ a. Saturday morning.

____ b. Saturday afternoon.

____ c. Sunday morning.

__X__ d. Sunday afternoon.

MASTERY REQUIREMENT: All correct

Indicate mastery on the student response sheet with a check.

THIRD LEVEL

III. COMPREHENSION

B. Sequence of Events

Name ____________________

Date ____________________

Mastery __________

DIRECTIONS: Read this story, then try to answer the questions below without looking back at the story.

Kay Baker and her dad put in a full day of work on Saturday fencing in the back yard. Then Sunday afternoon they worked until nearly dark building a doghouse. Now Prince had a safe place to play and a dry place to sleep.

Kay found an article in a book about dogs like Prince. He was a German Shepherd. They make good playmates for children, but are also excellent watchdogs and fighters when they need to be.

Prince is small now because he is just a puppy. He can almost crawl through the fence. When he grows up, though, he will be a large dog. Some German Shepherds weigh as much as a hundred pounds. He will be a good pet and also a useful and brave watchdog.

1. When did the Baker family get Prince?

____ a. When they saw how he could fight.

____ b. When he was grown.

____ c. When he was little.

2. The first night Prince could sleep in his new doghouse was

____ a. Saturday

____ b. Sunday

3. According to the story, Kay and her dad finished working

____ a. Saturday morning.

____ b. Saturday afternoon.

____ c. Sunday morning.

____ d. Sunday afternoon.

THIRD LEVEL

III. COMPREHENSION C. Can Draw Logical Conclusions

OBJECTIVE: The student will draw logical conclusions.

DIRECTIONS: Read this story, then answer the question that follows it.

"We need to stop soon for gasoline," Dad said as we neared the town where Grandmother lived. "Look, the needle is on empty. Maybe we can make it to her house. If we can, we'll get gas when we leave."

We drove on and, sure enough, we made it to Grandmother's house without running out of gas. We stayed and stayed. We stayed much longer than we had intended to. In fact, it was nearly midnight when we started getting ready to leave.

Suddenly Dad exclaimed, "You know, we may have a problem. It is a lot later than I thought we would be leaving."

Why is Dad worried about how late it is? Lateness may make it difficult to find an open gas station.

MASTERY REQUIREMENT: Correct response

Indicate mastery on the student response sheet with a check.

THIRD LEVEL

III. COMPREHENSION

C. Can Draw Logical Conclusions

Name ______________________________

Date ______________________________

Mastery ____________

DIRECTIONS: Read this story, then answer the question that follows it.

"We need to stop soon for gasoline," Dad said as we neared the town where Grandmother lived. "Look, the needle is on empty. Maybe we can make it to her house. If we can, we'll get gas when we leave."

We drove on and, sure enough, we made it to Grandmother's house without running out of gas. We stayed and stayed. We stayed much longer than we had intended to. In fact, it was nearly midnight when we started getting ready to leave.

Suddenly Dad exclaimed, "You know, we may have a problem. It is a lot later than I thought we would be leaving."

Why is Dad worried about how late it is? ______________________________

____

THIRD LEVEL

III. COMPREHENSION D. Can See Relationships

OBJECTIVE: The student will be able to see relationships.

DIRECTIONS: Mark the *best* choice for each of the following.

1. One of the nice things trees do for us is give shade. It is very pleasant to rest in the shade of a tree on a

   ____ a. cloudy day.

   ____ b. cool day.

   __X__ c. hot day.

2. It is dark in here. Will you please turn on the

   ____ a. radio.

   __X__ b. light.

   ____ c. water.

3. "I guess we must be lost," Mom said. "I don't know which road to take at this corner." Dad suggested that we pull over and look at

   ____ a. the car.

   ____ b. the light.

   __X__ c. the map.

4. "Hurry, Bob, or we are going to be

   __X__ a. late."

   ____ b. tired."

   ____ c. angry."

MASTERY REQUIREMENT: All correct

Indicate mastery on the student response sheet with a check.

THIRD LEVEL

III. COMPREHENSION

D. Can See Relationships

Name ______________________

Date ______________________

Mastery __________

DIRECTIONS: Mark the *best* choice for each of the following.

1. One of the nice things trees do for us is give shade. It is very pleasant to rest in the shade of a tree on a

____ a. cloudy day.

____ b. cool day.

____ c. hot day.

2. It is dark in here. Will you please turn on the

____ a. radio.

____ b. light.

____ c. water.

3. "I guess we must be lost," Mom said. "I don't know which road to take at this corner." Dad suggested that we pull over and look at

____ a. the car.

____ b. the light.

____ c. the map.

4. "Hurry, Bob, or we are going to be

____ a. late."

____ b. tired."

____ c. angry."

THIRD LEVEL

III. COMPREHENSION E. Can Predict Outcomes

OBJECTIVE: The student will be able to predict outcomes.

DIRECTIONS: Read the two short stories on this page, then write your own ending to each story.

Beth was tired. She had run all the way to the bus stop because she was afraid she was going to miss her school bus. When she got there the bus was not even in sight. "Whew!" she panted, "I'm glad I can rest here on the bench for a little while." She sat down on the bench, not noticing how bright and shiny it looked.

(After she had been seated for a little while, she felt something funny. She was sort of sticking to the bench. Suddenly she saw a sign on the back of the bench. The sign said, WET PAINT.)

Frank was happy to receive a ten dollar bill from his uncle as a birthday present. For days, he thought about what to buy with the money. Finally, he decided to buy a game he saw advertised in the newspaper. Frank put the ten dollar bill into the pocket of his old jacket when his mother said they were ready to go shopping.

(At the store, Frank found the game he wanted and took it to the counter to pay for it. When he reached into his pocket for the money, he was shocked to find that the pocket had a hole in it and the ten dollar bill was not there.)

MASTERY REQUIREMENT: Teacher judgment (This is an open-ended exercise. Any answer the student writes that makes sense is acceptable.)

Indicate mastery on the student response sheet with a check.

THIRD LEVEL

III. COMPREHENSION

E. Can Predict Outcomes

Name ______________________________

Date ______________________________

Mastery ___________

DIRECTIONS: Read the two short stories on this page, then write your own ending to each story.

Beth was tired. She had run all the way to the bus stop because she was afraid she was going to miss her school bus. When she got there the bus was not even in sight. "Whew!" she panted, "I'm glad I can rest here on the bench for a little while." She sat down on the bench, not noticing how bright and shiny it looked.

____

____

____

____

Frank was happy to receive a ten dollar bill from his uncle as a birthday present. For days, he thought about what to buy with the money. Finally, he decided to buy a game he saw advertised in the newspaper. Frank put the ten dollar bill into the pocket of his old jacket when his mother said they were ready to go shopping.

____

____

____

____

THIRD LEVEL

III. COMPREHENSION F. Following Printed Directions

OBJECTIVE: The student can follow printed directions.

DIRECTIONS:
1. Draw a circle around all the capital vowels.
2. Underline the first and last letters in the row of small letters.
3. Draw a circle around the 4th, 7th, and 8th letters in the bottom row.
4. In these blanks, write words which begin with the middle or center letter in each row.

(word beginning with a g)

(word beginning with a t)

(A) B C D (E) F G H (I) J K L M

n o p (q) r s (t) (u) v w x y z

MASTERY REQUIREMENT: All correct

Indicate mastery on the student response sheet with a check.

THIRD LEVEL

III. COMPREHENSION

F. Following Printed Directions

Name ______________________________

Date ______________________________

Mastery ___________

DIRECTIONS:

1. Draw a circle around all the capital vowels.

2. Underline the first and last letters in the row of small letters.

3. Draw a circle around the 4th, 7th, and 8th letters in the bottom row.

4. In these blanks, write words which begin with the middle or center letter in each row.

____

____

A B C D E F G H I J K L M

n o p q r s t u v w x y z

THIRD LEVEL

III. COMPREHENSION G. Definite Purpose 1. Pleasure

OBJECTIVE: The student reads for pleasure.

DIRECTIONS:

Ask the student to recall a story in a magazine or a novel which he or she has read with enjoyment recently. Do this periodically, insuring each time that the reading reported is not reading done in connection with a school assignment, but reading selected voluntarily and for pleasure.

MASTERY REQUIREMENT: Evidence that student reads for pleasure

Indicate mastery on the student response sheet with a check.

THIRD LEVEL

III. COMPREHENSION

G. Definite Purpose

1. Pleasure

Name ______________________________

Date ______________________________

Mastery ___________

Comment: ____

____

THIRD LEVEL

III. COMPREHENSION G. Definite Purpose 2. Answer question

OBJECTIVE: The student will read for the purpose of obtaining an answer to a question.

DIRECTIONS: Write a question in the blank on the student response sheet. Ask the student to read some source (you may suggest some sources that you know are available) where the answer will be found and answer the question on the sheet.

Suggestions: What kind of wood is used in making baseball bats?

Where do most of the diamonds in the world come from?

What was the first college in the United States?

What is the difference between horses and mules?

MASTERY REQUIREMENT: Obtaining an answer to the question assigned

Indicate mastery on the student response sheet with a check.

THIRD LEVEL

III. COMPREHENSION

G. Definite Purpose

2. Answer question

Name ______________________

Date ______________________

Mastery __________

Question: ____

____

Answer: ____

____

____

Source of Answer: ____

____

Teacher Comment: ____

____

THIRD LEVEL

III. COMPREHENSION G. Definite Purpose 3. General idea of content

OBJECTIVE: The student will be able to read to obtain a general idea of content.

DIRECTIONS: Select short to medium-length articles from newspapers, magazines, elementary encylopedias, etc. Hand the article to the student. Vary them frequently to avoid familiarity.

SAY: You will not have enough time to read this word for word. Just scan through it long enough to find out what it is about and some of the most important things it says.

Give the student about one-fourth of the time that would be necessary to read the entire selection in detail.

SAY: Now stop and tell me what you know about the article you looked at.

MASTERY REQUIREMENT: Teacher judgment of ability to relate general content

Indicate mastery on the student response sheet with a check.

THIRD LEVEL

III. COMPREHENSION

G. Definite Purpose

3. General idea of content

Name ______________________________

Date ______________________________

Mastery __________

Comment: ____

____

THIRD LEVEL

III. COMPREHENSION H. Classifying Items

OBJECTIVE: The student will classify items into appropriate categories.

DIRECTIONS: Some of the things in this list are necessary for you to have in order to live. Others are pleasant or good to have, but not necessary for life. Write them in the proper column.

		Necessary	Good to Have
1.	books		books
2.	air	air	
3.	food	food	
4.	dog		dog
5.	bicycle		bicycle
6.	water	water	
7.	toys		toys

DIRECTIONS: Here is a list of foods. Think of two columns you can make from the list. Put a heading on the top line above each column, then write each food item in the proper column.

		Meats	Vegetables
1.	pork chop	pork chop	
2.	spinach		spinach
3.	drumstick	drumstick	
4.	steak	steak	
5.	asparagus		asparagus
6.	sausage	sausage	
7.	cabbage		cabbage
8.	bacon	bacon	

MASTERY REQUIREMENT: All correct

Indicate mastery on the student response sheet with a check.

THIRD LEVEL

III. COMPREHENSION

H. Classifying Items

Name ____________________

Date ____________________

Mastery __________

DIRECTIONS: Some of the things in this list are necessary for you to have in order to live. Others are pleasant or good to have, but not necessary for life. Write them in the proper column.

	Necessary	Good to Have
1. books	________	________
2. air	________	________
3. food	________	________
4. dog	________	________
5. bicycle	________	________
6. water	________	________
7. toys	________	________

DIRECTIONS: Here is a list of foods. Think of two columns you can make from the list. Put a heading on the top line above each column, then write each food item in the proper column.

	________	________
1. pork chop	________	________
2. spinach	________	________
3. drumstick	________	________
4. steak	________	________
5. asparagus	________	________
6. sausage	________	________
7. cabbage	________	________
8. bacon	________	________

THIRD LEVEL

III. COMPREHENSION I. Use of Index

OBJECTIVE: The student will know how to use an index.

DIRECTIONS: Write TRUE or FALSE by each of these statements.

false 1. The index is usually near the front of the book.

true 2. The index lists items in alphabetical order.

true 3. The index lists all pages on which a topic is mentioned.

false 4. The index lists the title of each chapter.

false 5. The index lists items in order of page number.

true 6. The index is near the back of the book.

Use this short index to a health book to answer the questions below:

Accident prevention, 59-60, 85, 141-143, 224-225

Blood
Amount in body, 215
Circulation of, 56, 75-77, 162, 194

Bones
Growth of, 120-121, 244-245
In skeleton, 108, 110

Breathing
How you breathe, 113, 208-210

Hands
Bones of, 112

Hearing, sense of, 23, 24, 27, 37-38
Heart
Care of, 132, 198, 216

Safety
Avoiding burns, 85
Avoiding falls, 141-143
Senses (see Hearing, Sight, Smell, Taste, Touch)
Sight, sense of, 23, 24, 26, 28-30
Smell, sense of, 23, 24, 27, 44-46

Taste, sense of, 18, 23, 24, 27, 44
Touch, sense of, 23, 24, 27, 48

1. On what page would you look to find how many pints of blood are in your body? 215
2. How many pages would you need to read to find out all about your ears and how they work? 5
3. How many pages tell you about how to avoid hurting yourself by accidentally falling? 3
4. On what page would you look to find out about the bones in your hands? 112
5. What page would tell you how to avoid burns? 85
6. How many pages tell you about how you breathe? 4

MASTERY REQUIREMENT: 4 correct responses

Indicate mastery on the student response sheet with a check.

THIRD LEVEL

III. COMPREHENSION

I. Use of Index

Name ____________________

Date ____________________

Mastery __________

DIRECTIONS: Write TRUE or FALSE by each of these statements.

__________ 1. The index is usually near the front of the book.

__________ 2. The index lists items in alphabetical order.

__________ 3. The index lists all pages on which a topic is mentioned.

__________ 4. The index lists the title of each chapter.

__________ 5. The index lists items in order of page number.

__________ 6. The index is near the back of the book.

Use this short index to a health book to answer the questions below:

Accident prevention, 59-60, 85, 141-143, 224-225
Blood
  Amount in body, 215
  Circulation of, 56, 75-77, 162, 194
Bones
  Growth of, 120-121, 244-245
  In skeleton, 108, 110
Breathing
  How you breathe, 113, 208-210
Hands
  Bones of, 112
Hearing, sense of, 23, 24, 27, 37-38
Heart
  Care of, 132, 198, 216
Safety
  Avoiding burns, 85
  Avoiding falls, 141-143
Senses (see Hearing, Sight, Smell, Taste, Touch)
Sight, sense of, 23, 24, 26, 28-30
Smell, sense of, 23, 24, 27, 44-46
Taste, sense of, 18, 23, 24, 27, 44
Touch, sense of, 23, 24, 27, 48

1. On what page would you look to find how many pints of blood are in your body? __________

2. How many pages would you need to read to find out all about your ears and how they work? __________

3. How many pages tell you about how to avoid hurting yourself by accidentally falling? __________

4. On what page would you look to find out about the bones in your hands? __________

5. What page would tell you about how to avoid burns? __________

6. How many pages tell you about how you breathe? __________

THIRD LEVEL

III. COMPREHENSION J. Alphabetizing (2-letter)

OBJECTIVE: The student will alphabetize words using two-letter discrimination.

DIRECTIONS: Write these words in alphabetical order in the second column.

1.	seltzer	amorous
2.	migrant	awkward
3.	awkward	epic
4.	filch	filch
5.	symptom	formicary
6.	zinc	harpy
7.	xylem	migrant
8.	amorous	penguin
9.	epic	seltzer
10.	harpy	symptom
11.	zany	xylem
12.	formicary	zany
13.	penguin	zinc

MASTERY REQUIREMENT: All correct

Indicate mastery on the student response sheet with a check.

THIRD LEVEL

III. COMPREHENSION

J. Alphabetizing (2-letter)

Name ______________________

Date ______________________

Mastery __________

DIRECTIONS: Write these words in alphabetical order in the second column.

1. seltzer ______________
2. migrant ______________
3. awkward ______________
4. filch ______________
5. symptom ______________
6. zinc ______________
7. xylem ______________
8. amorous ______________
9. epic ______________
10. harpy ______________
11. zany ______________
12. formicary ______________
13. penguin ______________

THIRD LEVEL

III. COMPREHENSION   K. Skimming

OBJECTIVE: The student will know the technique of skimming.

DIRECTIONS: Make a copy of the student response sheet and direct the student as follows.

SAY: I am going to hand you a sheet of paper face down. When I say GO, turn it over and follow the directions at the top of the page just as quickly as you can.

STUDENT DIRECTIONS: Read these paragraphs as quickly as you can, then answer the two questions about them.

In the early history of the West, buffalo meat was an important food for both the settlers and the Indians. Many buffalo roamed over the country in large herds. But as more settlers came and more buffalo were killed for food, the buffalo herds became smaller and smaller. At last there were only a few small herds left.

Then some people began to raise buffalo. Today, buffalo are raised on ranches in the same way as cattle. Some stores sell buffalo steaks, roasts, and ground meat. Many people think buffalo meat tastes just like beef. In some parts of the country, there are restaurants that serve special dishes made of buffalo meat. There is even a buffalo cookbook.

1. Who ate buffalo meat in the early West? settlers

Indians

2. What does buffalo meat taste like? beef

MASTERY REQUIREMENT: Completion in less than 30 seconds

Indicate mastery on the student response sheet with a check.

THIRD LEVEL

III. COMPREHENSION

K. Skimming

Name ______________________

Date ______________________

Mastery __________

DIRECTIONS: Read these paragraphs as quickly as you can, then answer the two questions about them.

In the early history of the West, buffalo meat was an important food for both the settlers and the Indians. Many buffalo roamed over the country in large herds. But as more settlers came and more buffalo were killed for food, the buffalo herds became smaller and smaller. At last there were only a few small herds left.

Then some people began to raise buffalo. Today, buffalo are raised on ranches in the same way as cattle. Some stores sell buffalo steaks, roasts, and ground meat. Many people think buffalo meat tastes just like beef. In some parts of the country, there are restaurants that serve special dishes made of buffalo meat. There is even a buffalo cookbook.

1. Who ate buffalo meat in the early West? ______________________

____

2. What does buffalo meat taste like? ______________________

THIRD LEVEL

III. COMPREHENSION L. Sources of Information

OBJECTIVE: The student will correctly choose the most efficient source to find various types of information.

DIRECTIONS: You have the following items in which to find information:

1. Dictionary
2. Encyclopedia
3. Today's newspaper
4. Almanac
5. Road map

A science book with a

6. Glossary
7. Index

Which of these would be the best place to look first for the following information? Write the number in the blank.

a. Is there likely to be rain tomorrow? 3

b. The life story of Ben Franklin 2

c. The meaning of an unfamiliar word you find in your science lesson 6

d. The towns you go through traveling from Madison to Clinton 5

e. Information about blood pressure written in words you can understand 7

f. The batting champion of the National League in 1954 4

g. What the word "amphibian" means 1

h. What science experiments were perfected by Madame Curie? 2

i. The distance from Missouri to New Mexico 5

j. What special sales are ongoing at the grocery store? 3

MASTERY REQUIREMENT: 8 correct responses

Indicate mastery on the student response sheet with a check.

THIRD LEVEL

III. COMPREHENSION

L. Sources of Information

Name ____________________

Date ____________________

Mastery __________

DIRECTIONS: You have the following items in which to find information.

1. Dictionary
2. Encyclopedia
3. Today's newspaper
4. Almanac
5. Road map

A science book with a
6. Glossary
7. Index

Which of these would be the best place to look first for the following information? Write the number in the blank.

a. Is there likely to be rain tomorrow? __________

b. The life story of Ben Franklin __________

c. The meaning of an unfamiliar word you find in your science lesson __________

d. The towns you go through traveling from Madison to Clinton __________

e. Information about blood pressure written in words you can understand __________

f. The batting champion of the National League in 1954 __________

g. What the word "amphibian" means __________

h. What science experiments were perfected by Madame Curie? __________

i. The distance from Missouri to New Mexico __________

j. What special sales are ongoing at the grocery store? __________

THIRD LEVEL

III. COMPREHENSION M. Use of Maps and Charts

OBJECTIVE: The student will use maps and charts.

DIRECTIONS: Secure several copies of road maps of your state. Hand a map to the student.

SAY:

1. Show me our town on the map.
2. Show me the capital of our state on the map.
3. Show me the difference in the numbers on the map that show distance and the ones that are state and US highway numbers. (Refer the student to the legend for help, if needed.)
4. What neighboring state do we live closest to?
5. What highway would we get on to go there and what direction would we go?
6. Show me how we can get an idea of how large a city is by looking at the map.
7. Now turn to the highway mileage chart. Tell me how many miles it is from ________ to ________. (Be sure you are using towns listed on the chart.)

MASTERY REQUIREMENT: 5 correct responses

Indicate mastery on the student response sheet with a check.

THIRD LEVEL

III. COMPREHENSION

M. Use of Maps and Charts

Name ____________________

Date ____________________

Mastery __________

Check successful responses:

____ 1. Our town

____ 2. Capital

____ 3. Distance and highway numbers

____ 4. Neighboring state

____ 5. Highway number and direction

____ 6. Size of cities

____ 7. Mileage chart

THIRD LEVEL

IV. ORAL AND SILENT READING A. Oral Reading 1. Reads with expression

OBJECTIVE: The student will read with expression.

DIRECTIONS: Read this story aloud.

"Isn't that something unlucky, now!" Becky complained. "I spent all my homework time last night working on this long page of math problems. Look! There are forty blasted problems on the page, and I struggled through every one of them. Why, I didn't even get any help from mother! And now, after I get to school today, what happens? Joe tells me we were supposed to work page 95 in the math workbook, not the textbook. Oh! That is disgusting. The workbook page we were supposed to do has six little problems on it. I could have watched my favorite TV program instead of spending all that time on homework."

MASTERY REQUIREMENT: A rating of "Fair" or better (Teacher judgment)

Indicate mastery on the student response sheet with a check.

THIRD LEVEL

IV. ORAL AND SILENT READING

A. Oral Reading

1. Reads with expression

Name ____________________

Date ____________________

Mastery __________

DIRECTIONS: Read this story aloud.

"Isn't that something unlucky, now!" Becky complained. "I spent all my homework time last night working on this long page of math problems. Look! There are forty blasted problems on the page, and I struggled through every one of them. Why, I didn't even get any help from mother! And now, after I get to school today, what happens? Joe tells me we were supposed to work page 95 in the math workbook, not the textbook. Oh! That is disgusting. The workbook page we were supposed to do has six little problems on it. I could have watched my favorite TV program instead of spending all that time on homework."

Teacher rating: ____ Excellent

____ Good

____ Fair

____ Poor

Comment: ____

____

THIRD LEVEL

IV. ORAL AND SILENT READING   A. Oral Reading   2. Comprehends material read aloud

OBJECTIVE: The student will comprehend material read aloud.

DIRECTIONS: Make a copy of the reading selection on the following page, hand the sheet to the student, and have the student return the sheet to you after he/she has read the passage.

STUDENT DIRECTIONS: Read this paragraph aloud.

Do you know anyone who has hay fever? From the name of this ailment, you might think it causes people who have it to have fever. This is not usually true. Although it causes many problems, very seldom is fever one of them. Hay fever is what is called an allergy. People who have it are allergic to the pollen that is produced by some kinds of plants. Because of this, they usually are affected about the same season of the year each year. When they breathe air with pollen in it, they sneeze, their nose gets runny, and their eyes water and stay red and itchy. Luckily, for most people these conditions last only a short time each year.

(Continued on page 130.)

DIRECTIONS: Read this paragraph aloud.

Do you know anyone who has hay fever? From the name of this ailment, you might think it causes people who have it to have fever. This is not usually true. Although it causes many problems, very seldom is fever one of them. Hay fever is what is called an allergy. People who have it are allergic to the pollen that is produced by some kinds of plants. Because of this, they usually are affected about the same season of the year each year. When they breathe air with pollen in it, they sneeze, their nose gets runny, and their eyes water and stay red and itchy. Luckily, for most people these conditions last only a short time each year.

DIRECTIONS: After obtaining the reading passage from the student, give the student the student response sheet.

STUDENT DIRECTIONS: Answer these questions about the passage you just read.

1. Does hay fever get its name because it causes most people to have high fever? ___no___

2. Are most people who have hay fever bothered by it all year? ___no___

3. When people with hay fever breathe air with pollen in it, what does it do to them? ___causes sneezing, runny nose, watery eyes, red eyes, itching eyes.___

MASTERY REQUIREMENT: Correct responses on Nos. 1 and 2; at least two conditions named on No. 3

Indicate mastery on the student response sheet with a check.

THIRD LEVEL

IV. ORAL AND SILENT READING

A. Oral Reading

2. Comprehends material read aloud

Name ______________________________

Date ______________________________

Mastery ___________

DIRECTIONS: Answer these questions about the passage you just read.

1. Does hay fever get its name because it causes most people to have high fever? __________

2. Are most people who have hay fever bothered by it all year? __________

3. When people with hay fever breathe air with pollen in it, what does it do to them? ____

____

THIRD LEVEL

IV. ORAL AND SILENT READING B. Silent Reading 1. Finger pointing and lip movements

OBJECTIVE: The student will read silently without finger pointing or lip movement.

DIRECTIONS: Use any daily opportunities to appraise students on this objective. The appraisal should be made at a time when the student is unaware of being watched.

MASTERY REQUIREMENT: Demonstrated absence of mannerisms being appraised

Indicate mastery on the student response sheet with a check.

THIRD LEVEL

IV. ORAL AND SILENT READING

B. Silent Reading

1. Finger pointing and lip movements

Name ______________________

Date ______________________

Mastery __________

Comment: ____

____

____

IV. ORAL AND SILENT READING B. Silent Reading 2. Comprehends material read silently

OBJECTIVE: The student will comprehend material which has been read silently.

DIRECTIONS: Hand the student a copy of the following passage, page 135, then have the student return it to you after he/she has read the passage.

Do you get confused about the difference between a microscope and a telescope? A microscope is used to make tiny things appear larger so we can study them in more detail and see things about them that we cannot see without the microscope. For example, a microscope can help us see tiny sea animals, the tiny cells which make up our bodies, and the beautiful designs of snowflakes.

A telescope is used to look at things that are a long way from us. It makes far-off things look as if they are very near. Using a telescope, scientists can study the moon, planets, and other bodies in space. Field glasses, or binoculars, that we use for seeing distant things here on earth are two telescopes mounted together.

Perhaps we can remember the difference between a microscope and a telescope if we learn the meanings of two prefixes: "micro" means very, very small; "tele" means far, far away.

(Continued on page 136.)

DIRECTIONS: Read this silently.

Do you get confused about the difference between a microscope and a telescope? A microscope is used to make tiny things appear larger so we can study them in more detail and see things about them that we cannot see without the microscope. For example, a microscope can help us see tiny sea animals, the tiny cells which make up our bodies, and the beautiful designs of snowflakes.

A telescope is used to look at things that are a long way from us. It makes far-off things look as if they are very near. Using a telescope, scientists can study the moon, planets, and other bodies in space. Field glasses, or binoculars, that we use for seeing distant things here on earth are two telescopes mounted together.

Perhaps we can remember the difference between a microscope and a telescope if we learn the meanings of two prefixes: "micro" means very, very small; "tele" means far, far away.

DIRECTIONS: After obtaining the reading passage from the student, give him/her the student response sheet with the following questions.

1. If you wanted to examine a grain of sand very closely, would you use a telescope or a microscope? microscope

2. Would you need a microscope or a telescope if you wanted to get a better look at the moon? telescope

3. What are field glasses, or binoculars, made of? telescopes

4. If you wanted to look at the colors of the planet Mars, would you use a microscope or telescope? telescope

5. Would you use a microscope or a telescope if you were studying the tiny cells that make up the human body? microscope

6. What does the prefix "micro" mean? very small (or similar answer)

7. What does the prefix "tele" mean? far away (or similar answer)

MASTERY REQUIREMENT: 5 correct responses

Indicate mastery on the student response sheet with a check.

THIRD LEVEL

IV. ORAL AND SILENT READING

B. Silent Reading

2. Comprehends material read silently

Name ______________________

Date ______________________

Mastery __________

DIRECTIONS: Answer these questions about the passage you just read.

1. If you wanted to examine a grain of sand very closely, would you use a telescope or a microscope? ________________

2. Would you need a microscope or a telescope if you wanted to get a better look at the moon? ________________

3. What are field glasses, or binoculars, made of? ________________

4. If you wanted to look at the colors of the planet Mars, would you use a microscope or telescope? ________________

5. Would you need a telescope or a microscope if you were studying the tiny cells that make up the human body? ________________

6. What does the prefix "micro"mean? ________________

7. What does the prefix ""tele" mean? ________________

THIRD LEVEL

IV. ORAL AND SILENT READING B. Silent Reading 3. Reads faster silently than orally

OBJECTIVE: The student will be able to read more rapidly silently than orally.

DIRECTIONS: Use an opportunity during a daily silent reading assignment to time the student in his silent reading of a page containing no pictures. The student should not be aware that an observation is occurring. Record the time between page turning on the student response sheet. At another time, have the student read orally from a page in the same book that also has no pictures, timing this reading. Likewise, record this time on the student response sheet.

MASTERY REQUIREMENT: Silent reading time shorter than oral

Indicate mastery on the student response sheet with a check.

THIRD LEVEL

IV. ORAL AND SILENT READING

B. Silent Reading

3. Reads faster silently than orally

Name ______________________________

Date ______________________________

Mastery __________

Number of seconds to read page orally ______________

Number of seconds to read page silently ______________

THIRD LEVEL

IV. ORAL AND SILENT READING   C. Listening   1. Comprehends material read by another

OBJECTIVE: The student will comprehend material read aloud by another.

DIRECTIONS: Listen as this is read aloud.

Is there an empty feeling in your school? Is something missing? We hope so because the Instructional Television Office has picked up the black-and-white television cameras from every school. These are going to be sold and the money used to purchase new color cameras.

Information about the color cameras, how they can be checked out, and how to use them, will be in your hands shortly.

Just as a word of early information—the color cameras will be light and easy to operate. However, they will only be available for three days at a time. A few black-and-white cameras will be retained to check out for extended periods of time.

Now answer the questions on your sheet.

1. What will be done with most of the old cameras? ___will be sold___

2. What is about to be bought? ___new or color cameras___

3. Has information already been sent out about how to use the new cameras? ___no___

4. What is the limit on how long the color cameras may be kept? ___three days___

5. What is being kept for use over longer periods of time?

   ___a few black-and-white cameras___

MASTERY REQUIREMENT: 4 correct responses

Indicate mastery on the student response sheet with a check.

THIRD LEVEL

IV. ORAL AND SILENT READING

C. Listening

1. Comprehends material read by another

Name ____________________

Date ____________________

Mastery __________

DIRECTIONS: Answer these questions about the information you just heard read.

1. What will be done with most of the old cameras?

____

2. What is about to be bought?

____

3. Has information already been sent out about how to use the new cameras?

____

4. What is the limit on how long the color cameras may be kept?

____

5. What is being kept for use over longer periods of time?

____

THIRD LEVEL

IV. ORAL AND SILENT READING   C. Listening   2. Can follow directions read aloud

OBJECTIVE: The student will follow directions read aloud.

DIRECTIONS: Listen closely and do what you are instructed to do.

1. Near the center of your student response sheet, write your name, last name first.
2. Just below that, write your date of birth this way: first the day, then the month spelled out in full, then the last two numerals of the year.
3. At the bottom right corner of the sheet, write our room number, which is ____.
4. Just on the left edge of your paper, about halfway down from the top, draw a circle about the size of a dime, and fill it in completely.

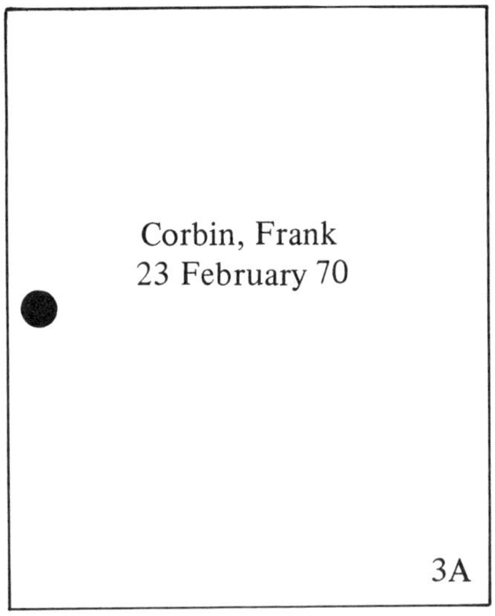

MASTERY REQUIREMENT: All correct (Don't be overly concerned about neatness, as children are working on unlined paper.)

Indicate mastery on the student response sheet with a check.

THIRD LEVEL

IV. ORAL AND SILENT READING

C. Listening

2. Can follow directions read aloud

Name ______________________

Date ______________________

Mastery __________

BARBE READING SKILLS CHECK LIST
THIRD LEVEL

(Last Name) ____________ (First Name) ____________ (Name of School) ____________

(Age) ____________ (Grade Placement) ____________ (Name of Teacher) ____________

I. Vocabulary:

A. Recognizes Dolch 220 Basic Sight Words

___ a
___ about
___ after
___ again
___ all
___ always
___ am
___ an
___ and
___ any
___ are
___ around
___ as
___ ask
___ at
___ ate
___ away
___ be
___ because
___ been
___ before
___ best
___ better
___ big
___ black
___ blue
___ both
___ bring
___ brown
___ but
___ buy
___ by
___ call
___ came
___ can
___ carry
___ clean
___ cold
___ come
___ could
___ cut
___ did
___ do
___ does

___ done
___ don't
___ down
___ draw
___ drink
___ eat
___ eight
___ every
___ fall
___ far
___ fast
___ find
___ first
___ five
___ fly
___ for
___ found
___ four
___ from
___ full
___ funny
___ gave
___ get
___ give
___ go
___ goes
___ going
___ good
___ got
___ green
___ grow
___ had
___ has
___ have
___ he
___ help
___ her
___ here
___ him
___ his
___ hold
___ hot
___ how
___ hurt

___ I
___ if
___ in
___ into
___ is
___ it
___ its
___ jump
___ just
___ keep
___ kind
___ know
___ laugh
___ let
___ light
___ like
___ little
___ live
___ long
___ look
___ made
___ make
___ many
___ may
___ me
___ much
___ must
___ my
___ myself
___ never
___ new
___ no
___ not
___ now
___ of
___ off
___ old
___ on
___ once
___ one
___ only
___ open
___ or
___ our

___ out
___ over
___ own
___ pick
___ play
___ please
___ pretty
___ pull
___ put
___ ran
___ read
___ red
___ ride
___ right
___ round
___ run
___ said
___ saw
___ say
___ see
___ seven
___ shall
___ she
___ show
___ sing
___ sit
___ six
___ sleep
___ small
___ so
___ some
___ soon
___ start
___ stop
___ take
___ tell
___ ten
___ thank
___ that
___ the
___ their
___ them
___ then
___ there

___ these
___ they
___ think
___ this
___ those
___ three
___ to
___ today
___ together
___ too
___ try
___ two
___ under
___ up
___ upon
___ us
___ use
___ very
___ walk
___ want
___ warm
___ was
___ wash
___ we
___ well
___ went
___ were
___ what
___ when
___ where
___ which
___ white
___ who
___ why
___ will
___ wish
___ with
___ work
___ would
___ write
___ yellow
___ yes
___ you
___ your

B. Word Meaning:

1. Comprehends and uses correctly the following words:

a. Function Words
—against
—also
—being
—during
—each
—end
—enough
—men
—more
—most
—other
—same
—should
—since
—such
—than
—though
—thought
—through
—while
—women

b. Direction Words
—around
—backward
—forward
—left
—right
—toward

c. Action Words
—carry
—draw
—kick
—push
—skate
—swim
—think
—throw
—travel

d. Forms of Address
—Miss
—Mr.
—Mrs.
—Ms.

e. Career Words
—artist
—factory
—lawyer
—mechanic
—money
—nurse
—office
—operator
—teacher
—training
—vocation

f. Color Words
—brown
—green
—orange
—purple

g. Metric Words
—centigrade
—gram
—liter
—meter

h. Curriculum Words
—add
—American
—country
—ecology
—even
—fall
—few
—greater
—less
—number
—odd
—seasons
—set
—space
—spring
—state
—subtract
—summer
—United States
—winter
—world

II. Word Analysis:

A. Refine phonics skills:
1. All initial consonant sounds
2. Short and long vowel sounds
3. Changes in words by:
   a. adding s, es, d, ed, ing, er, est
   b. dropping final e and adding ing
   c. doubling the consonant before adding ing
   d. changing y to i before adding es
4. Vowel rules
   a. vowel in one-syllable word is short
   b. vowel in syllable or word ending in e is long
   c. two vowels together, first is often long and second is silent
   d. vowel alone in word is short
5. C followed by i, e, y makes s sound
   C followed by a, o, u makes k sound
6. G followed by i, e, y makes j sound
   G followed by a, o, u makes guh sound
7. Silent letters in kn, wr, gn

B. Knows skills of:
1. Forming plurals
   by adding s, es, ies
   by changing f to v and adding es
2. Similarities of sound such as x and cks (box—blocks)
3. Can read Roman numerals I, V, X

C. Syllabication rules
1. There are usually as many syllables in a word as there are vowels
2. Where there is a single consonant between two vowels, the vowel goes with the first syllable (pu/pil)
3. When there is a double consonant, the syllable break is between the two consonants and one is silent (example: lit/tle)

D. Can hyphenate words using syllable rules
E. Understands use of primary accent mark
F. Knows to accent first syllable, unless it is a prefix, otherwise accent second syllable

III. Comprehension:

A. Can find main idea in story
B. Can keep events in proper sequence
C. Can draw logical conclusions
D. Is able to see relationships
E. Can predict outcomes
F. Can follow printed directions
G. Can read for a definite purpose:
1. for pleasure
2. to obtain answer to question
3. to obtain general idea of content

H. Classify items
I. Use index
J. Alphabetize words by first two letters
K. Knows technique of skimming
L. Can determine what source to obtain information (dictionary, encyclopedia, index, glossary, etc.)
M. Use maps and charts

IV. Oral and Silent Reading:

A. Oral Reading
1. Reads with expression
2. Comprehends material read aloud

B. Silent Reading
1. Reads silently without finger pointing, lip movements
2. Comprehends material read silently
3. Reads faster silently than orally

C. Listening
1. Comprehends material read aloud by another
2. Can follow directions read aloud

BARBE READING SKILLS CHECK LIST
THIRD LEVEL

(Last Name) (First Name) (Name of School)

(Age) (Grade Placement) (Name of Teacher)

I. Vocabulary:

A. Recognizes Dolch 220 Basic Sight Words

___ a	___ done	___ I	___ out	___ these
___ about	___ don't	___ if	___ over	___ they
___ after	___ down	___ in	___ own	___ think
___ again	___ draw	___ into	___ pick	___ this
___ all	___ drink	___ is	___ play	___ those
___ always	___ eat	___ it	___ please	___ three
___ am	___ eight	___ its	___ pretty	___ to
___ an	___ every	___ jump	___ pull	___ today
___ and	___ fall	___ just	___ put	___ together
___ any	___ far	___ keep	___ ran	___ too
___ are	___ fast	___ kind	___ read	___ try
___ around	___ find	___ know	___ red	___ two
___ as	___ first	___ laugh	___ ride	___ under
___ ask	___ five	___ let	___ right	___ up
___ at	___ fly	___ light	___ round	___ upon
___ ate	___ for	___ like	___ run	___ us
___ away	___ found	___ little	___ said	___ use
___ be	___ four	___ live	___ saw	___ very
___ because	___ from	___ long	___ say	___ walk
___ been	___ full	___ look	___ see	___ want
___ before	___ funny	___ made	___ seven	___ warm
___ best	___ gave	___ make	___ shall	___ was
___ better	___ get	___ many	___ she	___ wash
___ big	___ give	___ may	___ show	___ we
___ black	___ go	___ me	___ sing	___ well
___ blue	___ goes	___ much	___ sit	___ went
___ both	___ going	___ must	___ six	___ were
___ bring	___ good	___ my	___ sleep	___ what
___ brown	___ got	___ myself	___ small	___ when
___ but	___ green	___ never	___ so	___ where
___ buy	___ grow	___ new	___ some	___ which
___ by	___ had	___ no	___ soon	___ white
___ call	___ has	___ not	___ start	___ who
___ came	___ have	___ now	___ stop	___ why
___ can	___ he	___ of	___ take	___ will
___ carry	___ help	___ off	___ tell	___ wish
___ clean	___ her	___ old	___ ten	___ with
___ cold	___ here	___ on	___ thank	___ work
___ come	___ him	___ once	___ that	___ would
___ could	___ his	___ one	___ the	___ write
___ cut	___ hold	___ only	___ their	___ yellow
___ did	___ hot	___ open	___ them	___ yes
___ do	___ how	___ or	___ then	___ you
___ does	___ hurt	___ our	___ there	___ your

B. Word Meaning:

1. Comprehends and uses correctly the following words:

a. Function Words
—against —also —being —during —each —end —enough —men —more —most —other —same —should —since —such —than —though —thought —through —while —women

b. Direction Words
—around —backward —forward —left —right —toward

c. Action Words
—carry —draw —kick —push —skate —swim —think —throw —travel

d. Forms of Address
—Miss —Mr. —Mrs. —Ms.

e. Career Words
—artist —factory —lawyer —mechanic —money —nurse —office —operator —teacher —training —vocation

f. Color Words
—brown —green —orange —purple

g. Metric Words
—centigrade —gram —liter —meter

h. Curriculum Words
—add —American —country —ecology —even —fall —few —greater —less —number —odd —seasons —set —space —spring —state —subtract —summer —United States —winter —world

II. Word Analysis:

A. Refine phonics skills:
1. All initial consonant sounds
2. Short and long vowel sounds
3. Changes in words by:
   a. adding s, es, d, ed, ing, er, est
   b. dropping final e and adding ing
   c. doubling the consonant before adding ing
   d. changing y to i before adding es
4. Vowel rules
   a. vowel in one-syllable word is short
   b. vowel in syllable or word ending in e is long
   c. two vowels together, first is often long and second is silent
   d. vowel alone in word is short
5. C followed by i, e, y makes s sound
   C followed by a, o, u makes k sound
6. G followed by i, e, y makes j sound
   G followed by a, o, u makes guh sound
7. Silent letters in kn, wr, gn

B. Knows skills of:
1. Forming plurals
   by adding s, es, ies
   by changing f to v and adding es
2. Similarities of sound such as x and cks (box—blocks)
3. Can read Roman numerals I, V, X

C. Syllabication rules
1. There are usually as many syllables in a word as there are vowels
2. Where there is a single consonant between two vowels, the vowel goes with the first syllable (pu/pil)
3. When there is a double consonant, the syllable break is between the two consonants and one is silent (example: lit/tle)

D. Can hyphenate words using syllable rules
E. Understands use of primary accent mark
F. Knows to accent first syllable, unless it is a prefix, otherwise accent second syllable

III. Comprehension:

A. Can find main idea in story
B. Can keep events in proper sequence
C. Can draw logical conclusions
D. Is able to see relationships
E. Can predict outcomes
F. Can follow printed directions
G. Can read for a definite purpose:
1. for pleasure
2. to obtain answer to question
3. to obtain general idea of content

H. Classify items
I. Use index
J. Alphabetize words by first two letters
K. Knows technique of skimming
L. Can determine what source to obtain information (dictionary, encyclopedia, index, glossary, etc.)
M. Use maps and charts

IV. Oral and Silent Reading:

A. Oral Reading
1. Reads with expression
2. Comprehends material read aloud

B. Silent Reading
1. Reads silently without finger pointing, lip movements
2. Comprehends material read silently
3. Reads faster silently than orally

C. Listening
1. Comprehends material read aloud by another
2. Can follow directions read aloud

BARBE READING SKILLS CHECK LIST
THIRD LEVEL

(Last Name) (First Name) (Name of School)

(Age) (Grade Placement) (Name of Teacher)

I. Vocabulary:

A. Recognizes Dolch 220 Basic Sight Words

___ a	___ done	___ I	___ out	___ these
___ about	___ don't	___ if	___ over	___ they
___ after	___ down	___ in	___ own	___ think
___ again	___ draw	___ into	___ pick	___ this
___ all	___ drink	___ is	___ play	___ those
___ always	___ eat	___ it	___ please	___ three
___ am	___ eight	___ its	___ pretty	___ to
___ an	___ every	___ jump	___ pull	___ today
___ and	___ fall	___ just	___ put	___ together
___ any	___ far	___ keep	___ ran	___ too
___ are	___ fast	___ kind	___ read	___ try
___ around	___ find	___ know	___ red	___ two
___ as	___ first	___ laugh	___ ride	___ under
___ ask	___ five	___ let	___ right	___ up
___ at	___ fly	___ light	___ round	___ upon
___ ate	___ for	___ like	___ run	___ us
___ away	___ found	___ little	___ said	___ use
___ be	___ four	___ live	___ saw	___ very
___ because	___ from	___ long	___ say	___ walk
___ been	___ full	___ look	___ see	___ want
___ before	___ funny	___ made	___ seven	___ warm
___ best	___ gave	___ make	___ shall	___ was
___ better	___ get	___ many	___ she	___ wash
___ big	___ give	___ may	___ show	___ we
___ black	___ go	___ me	___ sing	___ well
___ blue	___ goes	___ much	___ sit	___ went
___ both	___ going	___ must	___ six	___ were
___ bring	___ good	___ my	___ sleep	___ what
___ brown	___ got	___ myself	___ small	___ when
___ but	___ green	___ never	___ so	___ where
___ buy	___ grow	___ new	___ some	___ which
___ by	___ had	___ no	___ soon	___ white
___ call	___ has	___ not	___ start	___ who
___ came	___ have	___ now	___ stop	___ why
___ can	___ he	___ of	___ take	___ will
___ carry	___ help	___ off	___ tell	___ wish
___ clean	___ her	___ old	___ ten	___ with
___ cold	___ here	___ on	___ thank	___ work
___ come	___ him	___ once	___ that	___ would
___ could	___ his	___ one	___ the	___ write
___ cut	___ hold	___ only	___ their	___ yellow
___ did	___ hot	___ open	___ them	___ yes
___ do	___ how	___ or	___ then	___ you
___ does	___ hurt	___ our	___ there	___ your

B. Word Meaning:

1. Comprehends and uses correctly the following words:

a. Function Words
—against
—also
—being
—during
—each
—end
—enough
—men
—more
—most
—other
—same
—should
—since
—such
—than
—though
—thought
—through
—while
—women

b. Direction Words
—around
—backward
—forward
—left
—right
—toward

c. Action Words
—carry
—draw
—kick
—push
—skate
—swim
—think
—throw
—travel

d. Forms of Address
—Miss
—Mr.
—Mrs.
—Ms.

e. Career Words
—artist
—factory
—lawyer
—mechanic
—money
—nurse
—office
—operator
—teacher
—training
—vocation

f. Color Words
—brown
—green
—orange
—purple

g. Metric Words
—centigrade
—gram
—liter
—meter

h. Curriculum Words
—add
—American
—country
—ecology
—even
—fall
—few
—greater
—less
—number
—odd
—seasons
—set
—space
—spring
—state
—subtract
—summer
—United States
—winter
—world

II. Word Analysis:

A. Refine phonics skills:
1. All initial consonant sounds
2. Short and long vowel sounds
3. Changes in words by:
   a. adding s, es, d, ed, ing, er, est
   b. dropping final e and adding ing
   c. doubling the consonant before adding ing
   d. changing y to i before adding es
4. Vowel rules
   a. vowel in one-syllable word is short
   b. vowel in syllable or word ending in e is long
   c. two vowels together, first is often long and second is silent
   d. vowel alone in word is short
5. C followed by i, e, y makes s sound
   C followed by a, o, u makes k sound
6. G followed by i, e, y makes j sound
   G followed by a, o, u makes guh sound
7. Silent letters in kn, wr, gn

B. Knows skills of:
1. Forming plurals
   by adding s, es, ies
   by changing f to v and adding es
2. Similarities of sound such as x and cks (box—blocks)
3. Can read Roman numerals I, V, X

C. Syllabication rules
1. There are usually as many syllables in a word as there are vowels
2. Where there is a single consonant between two vowels, the vowel goes with the first syllable (pu/pil)
3. When there is a double consonant, the syllable break is between the two consonants and one is silent (example: lit/tle)

D. Can hyphenate words using syllable rules
E. Understands use of primary accent mark
F. Knows to accent first syllable, unless it is a prefix, otherwise accent second syllable

III. Comprehension:

A. Can find main idea in story
B. Can keep events in proper sequence
C. Can draw logical conclusions
D. Is able to see relationships
E. Can predict outcomes
F. Can follow printed directions
G. Can read for a definite purpose:
1. for pleasure
2. to obtain answer to question
3. to obtain general idea of content
H. Classify items
I. Use index
J. Alphabetize words by first two letters
K. Knows technique of skimming
L. Can determine what source to obtain information (dictionary, encyclopedia, index, glossary, etc.)
M. Use maps and charts

IV. Oral and Silent Reading:

A. Oral Reading
1. Reads with expression
2. Comprehends material read aloud

B. Silent Reading
1. Reads silently without finger pointing, lip movements
2. Comprehends material read silently
3. Reads faster silently than orally

C. Listening
1. Comprehends material read aloud by another
2. Can follow directions read aloud